Contents

Dedication

To my Mom and Dad:
For your unconditional love
and believing I am more than I think I am.

To my wife Kristina:
For walking life's path hand in hand with me.

To our children, Colby, Linnea, and Magnus:
For giving me the best reason to want to continue winning.

Preface to the Second Edition

by Cary Mullen

INCREASING YOUR SALES, MAKING MORE MONEY, becoming a better leader, building stronger relationships, finding true love, enjoying life, believing in yourself, clarifying a higher purpose, and living with more energy are all benefits that readers have reported after applying the principles in *How to Win*.

Today's world economic climate has shifted from conditions that might be described as having been a gentle tail breeze on the bunny hill to what is now a head wind in an extreme sport that we didn't even sign up for! Two groups of people will emerge during this recession. There will be those that sit with their head in their hands—drifting, stalled, and stuck and then there will be those that choose to draw a line in the sand, take responsibility, maintain control, and remain accountable for their own lives and economic security.

In case you haven't received the memo, I'd recommend that you do all in your power to ensure you are a member of the second group. As a matter of fact, you may well be called upon to help lead it! And thank goodness you will be, because this chaotic world needs great leaders—*now*!

For all those of us who are ready to work hard and keep our nose to the proverbial grindstone, there are as many opportunities open to us now as there have ever been in the past. Granted, these opportunities will be different, but they are there to be found as surely as the sun comes up on my windowsill. In years to come, I believe that we will look back upon these next few years and recognize the rise of more iconic leaders than in the preceding decades. As a result, I think we will see the making of more millionaires and billionaires than ever. The journey ahead of us is not for the faint of heart (nor is it for those with a minimal work ethic). Now is the time for achievers! This is no time for any of us to hesitate or lose focus. We simply can't afford to get sloppy or let a 'good enough' mentality creep into our thinking (or the operation of our companies). The rest of the world might elect to freewheel but we can benefit through exercising our leadership skills and acting decisively.

In the current economic climate we're witnessing more fear and uncertainty than we have seen in more than 40 and perhaps as much as 70 years. In such extreme economic circumstances many will stumble, fall and fail, and yet others will prevail. How will those with the instinct and drive to win rise above their circumstances? They'll do it with optimism, an unwavering belief in themselves and through the application of five *Winning Secrets*™. In one way or another, individuals who consistently achieve the best results—regardless of their chosen profession—apply these same five principles to consistently establish and achieve sustainable goals and manifest a successful, winning life. This is my personal definition of winning— getting the results *you* want.

Over the past few years, it has been an honor to be invited to share my stories and strategies with hundreds of organizations and thousands of individuals around the world. In my life I have experienced times when conditions and circumstances have been extremely challenging: from placing last in my first World Cup Downhill race, to struggling with and recovering from three severe concussions, to setting the World Cup Downhill speed record of 97 mph in Kitzbüel Austria, to crashing into the net at the Olympic Games, to being at my wife's side during the delivery of our first born, to Winning a World Cup Downhill race, to his dream of building the best retirement resort in the world.

I feel I have been both blessed and cursed with a particular calling. For some reason I was meant to risk my life, to push the absolute extreme limits of human potential in order to find out how to succeed at the pinnacle in life—to be the best in the world. Why? I believe that I was called on to do these things so that I could share the outcomes and the lessons with you in this book. It has been difficult to write, but the good news is that it's easy to read. It doesn't matter if you are a multi-millionaire, a start-up entrepreneur, the CEO of a *Fortune 500* company, a stay-at-home parent, a salesperson, an athlete, an artist or an academic, this book can entertain you, inspire you and most importantly help you get more of the results that you want in your life.

Cary Mullen
Puerto Escondido, Mexico
March, 2009

Foreword

by Vince Poscente

W HENEVER HE EMBARKED UPON A NEW VENTURE, he was not among the best but he has always learned how to become one of the best. He was not born with a silver spoon in his mouth but managed to grow a personal fortune in just a short period of time. He was not necessarily among the most gifted but he has figured out how to win, over, over and over again.

The person I'm talking about is Cary Mullen.

In your own life, think of someone you know who has continually impressed you. You may have met this apparently ordinary person on an idle Tuesday and yet time has revealed that this person has some special qualities—among them, the ability to explore life to its fullest. Couple that ability with the attribute of contribution—leaving the metaphorical campsite better than he found it, and you have an extraordinary person. In my life, such a person is Cary Mullen.

I met Cary on a return visit to my former hometown, Calgary. He had retired from a successful skiing career and was moving on from his leadership development role with *Dale Carnegie Training*. Following a speech I had made at the Olympic Hall of Fame, at Canada Olympic Park, Cary pulled me aside to ask a question. In his humble way he wondered if I had any advice for him regarding the speaking business.

In the interim seven years, we have developed a wonderful personal and professional friendship. More importantly it's your turn to get to know Cary Mullen. He has recently written his first book and it could not be more appropriately named *How to Win: Achieving Your Goals in Extreme Conditions*.

I invite you to explore insights from his life.

As you immerse yourself in this book, you will read about a guy who went from the lowest ranked skier to two-time Olympian, North American Champion, and World Cup Champion. You will learn about some of his exceptional setbacks and challenges and how he ultimately turned them into winning situations. Cary's entry into in the speaking business was modest. However, he replicated his reach-the-top formula and found a way to win again. Successful Meetings Magazine has ranked Cary as one of the hottest speakers on the motivational circuit. In the world of real estate investment, Cary has out performed most of the competition. Before he turned 40, Cary had accumulated more than one hundred properties—among them, the famous beachfront paradise Casa Rubia as well as an extraordinary oceanfront development in the most pristine, hidden treasure of Mexico—Puerto Escondido.

Let me take the liberty of inviting Cary into your life.

He has a regular newsletter. You can sign up for that via his website **www.CaryMullen.com**. Heck, he could even be your neighbor at his Mexico paradise, Vivo Resorts. You can take a look at this stunning condominium development at **www.VivoResorts.com**.

The only decision you have to make is how earnestly you reach for the hand Cary is extending. Leverage his past and present pursuits. Become the kind of person who impresses and inspires others. Learn how to win—over, over and over again.

Vince Poscente
New York Times *Bestselling Author* – The Age of Speed
Olympian and Speaker Hall of Fame
October 2008
Dallas, Texas

Introduction

BEFORE WE GO ANY FURTHER, YOU MIGHT BE WONDERING, "What is winning and what can it do for me?" The truth is that by winning you can achieve anything you can imagine. Winning is simply achieving the results you desire. For you, winning could be increasing your sales figures, buying the new car you've had your eye on for the past year, or having more energy and passion in your life. It could be about establishing or expanding your legacy, improving the relationship you have with your children, or making more money. Winning is about success and is however YOU choose to define it. The best news of all is that winning can be learned and I can show you how. Winning isn't solely a matter of luck, of that I can assure you! Winning is about hard work, but it can be fun, and it is definitely a process that can be learned. Winning is something anyone can learn to accomplish and, in doing so, they can take their achievements to a whole new level! With the secrets I'll share in *How to Win*, it is a process that is entirely replicable!

You might be interested to learn that I have spent my entire life devoted to mastering the psychology and practices of winning. Much of what I learned is privileged information I gained over twenty years of competing in world-class professional sport, an

Winning is simply achieving the results you desire.

Winning is about success and is however you choose to define it.

arena exclusively created to focus on the art of winning. In this environment, competition is not merely encouraged, it is an absolutely necessity. Achievement in sport is clearly delineated and precisely measured—in alpine skiing, to the hundredth of a second—and a public declaration of winners and losers can always be expected. Professional athletes know something that the rest of the world rarely experiences: winning is as much about following a disciplined process as it is living into a way of being. What you see, as a spectator of World Cup skiing,

1

for example, is the 2-minute race. What I am going to share with you is everything that happens behind the scenes; everything that collectively makes the difference between an athlete placing first or last. Having worked my way up the ranks, I know what it is like to be both first and last, and what it takes to become a champion. I am excited to share with you these secrets of training and ritual which, if you incorporate them into your own life, will absolutely help you succeed and take your successes to an altogether higher level. The secrets contained within this book will help you, as they helped me, achieve your greatest dreams.

This book is an evolution of my work on understanding How to WIN. My work has resulted in uncovering five well-defined principles, the same five secrets I have shared in helping thousands of people experience a significant, quantum change in their lives.

How I share these principles, the five *Winning Secrets™*, is a bit different from most other books you may have read. When I began facilitating leadership development with *Dale Carnegie Training* and later, as a keynote speaker, I noticed that long after people had forgotten the theories and concepts I had taught them, they still remembered the stories I had shared. I can't tell you how many times I've run into former workshop participants who could still recall a story I had shared with them two or three, even five years earlier. Some of these people would tell me how a particular story had continued to influence how they looked at things or, better still, how they subsequently acted on things in their own life. I began to realize that there is something fundamentally powerful about a good story.

> *There is something fundamentally powerful about a good story.*

Nowadays, I am always on the look out for a good story because I know how influential they can be. Besides, for most of us, reading a story is a lot more fun than trying to remember a whole lot of dry facts and theory. In fact, I'm so hooked on stories that whenever I read a non-fiction book I'm quickly disappointed if I find there are no rich and vivid stories for me to learn from. That is why my book is different from many other books. *How to Win* is not a boring book filled with weighty philosophical theory. No way! It is a compilation of real-life short stories on winning, each of which has been written to help you achieve more success in your life.

You will read stories from my life, stories of failure and success, of heartache and passion. I wasn't always a published author. I certainly didn't grow up with a silver spoon in my mouth. I didn't start out as a World Cup champion or as a business leader. I haven't always been triumphant and, frankly, some of the stories within these pages were quite painful to recount. However, I share my stories with you as illustrations of what can happen when you apply my five *Winning Secrets*™ to your life. Using the same principles I am now sharing with you, I have achieved financial success, earning over a million dollars in three different industries, and have been blessed in accumulating a multi-million dollar net worth. We have our dream vacation home and winter retreat in the most amazing part of Mexico—Puerto Escondido. I am married to a wonderful woman Kristina, and we have three beautiful children, Colby, Linnea and Magnus. More importantly, we have a lifestyle that enables us to be actively involved in our children's and each other's lives. I'm not telling you any of this so that you can think, "How great for Cary." I am sharing these indicators of my success as evidence of how these secrets can help you achieve the same sort of success or, perhaps, greater success for yourself! I want you to achieve your greatest dreams!

The short stories in this book are both inspirational and instructive. While there is no single "right" way to read this book, if you are currently struggling with a problem in your life that is blocking your ability to succeed, you want to start by addressing that issue first. If you flip to the thematic story index at the back of the book, you'll find a list of common obstacles to winning, such as struggling with perfection, choosing the best opportunity, or knowing when to cut your losses. These common obstacles have been matched to a story (or stories) that speak directly to the issue or issues. These are the stories you'll want to get started with. As you read each story, try to imagine yourself in the situations I describe. Then think about how you can integrate and manifest the life lessons within each story in your own life. Collectively, I hope my stories will help you to see things differently than you did before and, if they do, that's great, but it's also not enough. The truth is

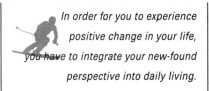

In order for you to experience positive change in your life, you have to integrate your new-found perspective into daily living.

that in order for you to experience positive change in your life, you have to integrate your new-found perspective into daily living. That's why, at the end of every story, I have provided some questions for you to think about. Your answers to these questions will provide you with an opportunity to achieve the success you have dreamed of and ultimately build a better life.

Having written this book, I'm committed to continuing to share my experiences with people like you who are focused on winning. If you are interested in receiving accounts of my most recent experiences and life lessons, I invite you to sign up for *Winning Insights*. By signing up, you will receive short stories, strategies and quick tips on winning every two weeks. Registering doesn't cost you anything other than a few minutes of your time. Visit **www.carymullen.com** to join us, and you will begin receiving new stories from me straight away. Just think, you can spend ten minutes with me every two weeks and significantly improve your life—and it's free!

The Five Winning Secrets™

While taking action is critical to living a winning life, action taken outside of a clear process and winning philosophy will keep you busy, but it is unlikely to get you where you really want to go. Living the principles embodied within my five *Winning Secrets*™ is the key to having a more successful life. In my experience, the more I've applied these five *Winning Secrets*™, the easier my life has become. Aligning your actions with these winning principles will become easier with practice. As you work through the short stories in this book, my hope is that your alignment of action with principle becomes second nature to you.

This book is divided into five sections; each section is devoted to one of the five *Winning Secrets*™. Each section begins with a brief overview of the secret before delving into stories that illustrate what the secret looks like in action. The short stories will help you to identify the common obstacles to winning that typically show up, as well as patterns of conditioning associated with them. You'll begin to understand the core beliefs and fears that for most of us get in the way of our living into that particular principle. More importantly, you'll be able to determine whether negative beliefs or fears are within you, and holding you back from greater success. Finally, you'll see how you can integrate the five *Winning Secrets*™ into your life.

Before we get started, I have a confession to make. When first I began to write this book, I had in my mind that it was going to be a "how to" book containing what I thought were the answers or solutions to leading a winning life. That's right—a series of concepts, models and theories laid out with thorough explanations that would have been a far bigger book than this. Sounds pretty boring, huh? In the end, that's what I thought too. That's why the manuscript for this book evolved to become one of short stories and questions designed to invite your own reflections and help you find the answers within yourself.

I am so committed to helping other people win that I couldn't let go of a nagging feeling that I needed to provide people with more. I wanted to share all that I have learned about winning over the past 20 years, and give more in-depth information about the five *Winning Secrets*™, as well as provide more exercises and coaching tips to assist readers in truly integrating the principles embodied in the five *Winning Secrets*™. I knew that a book just wasn't a sufficient response. Over two years, and with significant financial investment, together with my creative development team, I am pleased to announce that we have designed the *How to Win Success System*. This interactive, five-module, multimedia self-development program has been designed to help you achieve even more success. The system is not for the faint of heart. It is a comprehensive program of self-development intended to overhaul your entire life, eliminate negative habits and beliefs, and provide you with all of the tools you require in order to succeed. Why am I sharing this with you? Having purchased this book, it is reasonable to assume you are interested in learning How to Win. Because you have taken the first step, I am going to help you take the next several steps. By e-mailing me at **cary@carymullen.com** and requesting your How to WIN coupon, you will be eligible to purchase the *How to Win Success System* for $227 instead of the usual $297—a savings of $70. If you're serious about creating more enduring success and would like more information, visit us at **www.carymullen.com** and look under *How to Win Success System* to review the system for yourself.

OK, that's enough of my sales pitch. Here's a brief overview of the five *Winning Secrets*™ before you dive into the stories.

Secret #1: The Winning Process

Has there been a time in your life when you assumed that everything was going along just as it should be, only to be shocked by the unexpected loss of an important deal to a competitor or by being passed over for a promotion without warning? Secret #1 will ensure that this kind of experience doesn't happen to you again. This secret is a *Winning Process* that gives you a competitive edge by moving you to the top of your game and keeping you there. The *Winning Process* is a four-step method that will not only help you achieve your goals more quickly, it will teach you the same process used by top performers to consistently win. By reading the stories in this section, you'll see how building on your strengths and assessing your weaknesses can help you to regain both perspective and enthusiasm. You will be empowered by the clear roadmap for success that this process provides. Most importantly, you will start experiencing consistent and phenomenal success.

> *Building on your strengths and assessing your weaknesses can help you to regain both perspective and enthusiasm.*

Secret #2: Pick Your Line

What are your goals? Do you have a plan designed to achieve those goals? Have you allowed hurdles to block your intended path and impede your progress towards reaching your goals? Secret #2 is about the power of focus. At an early stage in my life, I made the mistake of trying to divide my focus. I wanted

Discover how to tap into your clarity and passion so that you can achieve better results.

to be the best at everything I turned my attention towards. In fact, I wanted to be an Olympic champion in two very different sports—ski racing and gymnastics. As you explore the secret of *picking your line*, I'll be sharing with you both the lessons I learned as a youngster who wanted it all, and those I learned later, as an adult, who sometimes let indecision cloud his focus. When you have read the stories in this section, you'll have discovered how to tap into your clarity and passion so that you can achieve better results. There are many life situations and consequent decisions we must make that can pull us away from our intended goals. In daily life, we can be faced with many distractions, not all of which are possible for us to avoid. How we handle such situations, decisions and distractions will directly affect how quickly we achieve our goals.

Secret #3: Lunge Forward

This powerful secret will help you overcome psychological barriers to success. Many times, after we have chosen a goal, we allow fear and indecision to block us from achieving the success we desire. Learning how to overcome fear is one of the greatest lessons I learned during my professional sports career. The success that I have today can be directly attributed to this lesson, Secret #3, and the approach that I developed to manage fear. *Lunging Forward* is the ability to overcome what I call, "the eleventh-hour voice of doubt." It is the ability to overcome all those negative thoughts in your head just before you're about to execute your plan of action, whether that is to pick up the phone and make the call, stand up to begin your presentation, or, as a skier, push through the starting gate. Overcoming the tendency to cave in to the negative attitude that performance stress presents ensures that you can execute your best performance and enhance your chances of success. When

> *Lunging forward means embracing your life today and making the most of who you are, what you are fully capable of doing, and maintaining a clear vision of who you are capable of becoming.*

you have read the stories in this section, you will be better able to identify your fears, assess risk versus rewards, and make proactive decisions as opposed to simply reacting out of fear. Lunging forward means embracing your life today and making the most of who you are, what you are fully capable of doing, and maintaining a clear vision of who you are capable of becoming. Lunging forward means taking risks and then realizing the rewards as you live your life to its fullest right here, today.

Secret #4: Be Resilient

How fast do you bounce back from adversity? Sure, it's normal, and to be expected, that we become frustrated from time to time with our present circumstances, especially when we've experienced a setback. But are there times when you feel stuck, when you repeatedly ask yourself "Why me?" as you think about how things ought to be? To win in life means that you will fail many times before you succeed. This is true for all of us, both for the Donald Trumps in this life as well as for you and me. The only difference between top performers and the rest of us is that top performers have learned to get back up from their failures more quickly. The purpose of Secret #4, is to be resilient, is to help you get unstuck when you're dwelling on a performance where you've experienced failure. This principle will help you to persevere through adversity and develop a stronger, more resilient belief in yourself following a setback. Mastering resilience will help you believe in and

> *The only difference between top performers and the rest of us is that top performers have learned to get back up from their failures more quickly.*

remain committed to your ultimate goals. In this section, I share stories with you from my darkest hours—from near-death concussions to accounts of some embarrassing failures, both private and very public. While setbacks are an inevitable part of life, it is how you react to these setbacks that defines who you are. Will you allow setbacks to define you, or will you embrace them as opportunities to learn, grow, and become more successful?

> *Surrounding yourself with the right people is fundamental to your ability to maintain your motivation and positive energy.*

Secret #5: Teamwork Wins

The final secret is about teamwork. Teamwork not only makes winning possible, it makes winning easier. Athletes rarely operate in isolation and are typically surrounded by a team. You have coaches, nutritionists, physical therapists and medical doctors, not to mention your teammates or the countless support staff who are all there to ensure you are able to perform at your very best. Surrounding yourself with the right people is fundamental to your ability to maintain your motivation and positive energy. The experience and assistance of others will not only optimize your chances of success, their involvement will help keep you on track during each step of the process towards success. When you seek out and learn from the experience of others, and look to leverage your success by using the knowledge and skills of others, then you will achieve success more quickly. Of course, it's always possible to try and achieve your goals by yourself. People do this all the time. However, I'm advocating that the ability to work with a team, Secret#5, will produce the results you desire more quickly and they will be all the more gratifying for having done so.

The stories in this section demonstrate that when you're able to harness the power of others, surround yourself with positive influences, and leverage a great support system, winning has a different meaning and takes on a whole new feeling.

I welcome you to the stories that will help you understand How to Win. I guarantee that if you take the time to read this collection of stories, personal recollections and insights, embrace the

> *When you seek out and learn from the experience of others, and look to leverage your success by using the knowledge and skills of others, then you will achieve success more quickly.*

questions presented at the end of each story, and incorporate the principles into your life, you will achieve the level of success that you are seeking. You will achieve your goals and you *will* win!

Decide now that you will no longer settle for anything less than what you really want in life. Choose to be fully alive, fully engaged, and step whole-heartedly into your winning life!

You were born with potential.
You were born with goodness and trust.
You were born with ideals and dreams.
You were born with greatness.
You were born with wings.
You are not meant for crawling, so don't.
You have wings.
Learn to use them and fly.

RUMI

1
The Winning Process

I F YOU HAVEN'T BEEN ABLE TO CONSISTENTLY GET THE RESULTS you
were looking for in the past, the reason is simple—you have never
been given the information that top performers know. You have
never been given the winning process. Instead of stumbling around in
the dark, experiencing random acts of success, there is a process that
can help you succeed more consistently. The process consists of four
proven steps that form a natural cycle. Achieving your goals with
greater consistency and superior results becomes possible as you follow
this clear roadmap. Embrace, practice, and implement these four steps
and you will be well on your way to achieving the success you have
been striving for.

What are the four steps in the *Winning Process*?

- Preparation
- Execution
- Assessment
- Rejuvenation

When I first created the *Winning Process*, I was convinced I had stumbled
upon something new and created an innovative model for success.
You might imagine my surprise when a colleague informed me that
this process was already a well-established performance cycle, mirroring
the work of D.A. Kolb (1984) and his cycle of experiential learning
(concrete experience [Execution], reflective observation [Assessment],
abstract conceptualization [Preparation], and active experimentation
[this is part Preparation and part Execution]). The major difference
between my model and Kolb's model is that the *Winning Process*
includes a stage of rejuvenation. I was disappointed to learn that what
I thought I had developed wasn't something entirely original. I also

realized the advantage I had uncovered in re-discovering this process: it had already been proven! It has already helped thousands of others achieve better results. How, then, can you fail if you also apply these same four steps?

Independently, each step is powerful and important. Put them together, and they are a model for success. Each step also plays a valuable part in the entire process and cannot be skipped. In fact, some steps may play a more important role than you have ever formerly realized.

As an athlete, I tracked how much time we spent in preparation, execution, assessment, and rejuvenation during our days, weeks, and months on the World Cup skiing circuit. It might surprise you to learn that we spent 40% of our time in preparation. That's a lot of time! While I don't necessarily subscribe to the belief that everyone should spend as much as 40% of their time in this phase of the cycle, I would ask you to calculate how much time you do spend in this vital area. In fact, I encourage you to look at how much time you spend in each of the four steps: preparation, execution, assessment, and rejuvenation. I also encourage you to take a hard look at the process, if any, you currently follow and see if you are overlooking or undervaluing any of these critical steps.

Preparation

Are you prepared to win? Preparation is key to success. Every day we're busy doing, doing, doing, yet so often we forget to allocate appropriate time to preparation. Preparation allows you to make the most of your current resources: your skills, knowledge, experience, and confidence. Preparation enables you to maximize your performance regardless of what is likely to happen. Preparation serves to reduce unnecessary risk and enables you to optimize your current resources.

> *The greatest tool that you can use is the one that professional athletes use—visualization.*

You've probably heard the cliché that you need to give 110% when you execute your performance; it is indeed a cliché! The reality is that if you were to make a total, 100% commitment when you prepare for anything, then the execution phase becomes much easier and significantly more enjoyable. It is vital that you allocate an appropriate amount of time for preparation.

So how do you prepare to win? The greatest tool that you can use is the one that professional athletes use—visualization. One of the best ways to prepare for anything is the process of creating mental images or models. It wasn't until much later in my career that I learned how valuable visualization and mental rehearsal could be. I believe this to be the greatest skill any professional athlete could teach you. As I improved my visualization skills, My performance level soared.

Execution

After you've undertaken your preparation, it is time to move into action. It is time to execute your performance!

The execution phase of the process is just that. It is the time when you make that phone call, make your presentation, move into action to execute and achieve your stated goal. This is the time when fear and doubt can creep into consciousness. The third winning secret, *Lunging Forward*, will help you mitigate those fears and be prepared to handle any hurdles that arise during the execution of your performance.

The execution of your goal should be a fun experience! Your goals are a reflection of who you are and what you love to do. For me, at one time, it was all about skiing. I loved skiing and to have had the level of success I eventually experienced, I needed to maintain sufficient passion and retain my

> *The execution phase can be broken down into three smaller steps. These are what I describe as 1) getting psyched, 2) doing it, and 3) being in flow.*

motivation to see me through the times of difficulty, discouragement, and failure. There were many such times, and I'll share some of these with you in the stories presented in this book. What pulled me through those trying times, most of the time, were both my passion for the sport and my passion for winning—for being the best!

> *The execution phase is about realizing your fears and overcoming them in order to direct all of your energy into your performance and performing that with a complete, conscious enjoyment of the moment.*

The execution phase can be broken down into three smaller steps. These are what I describe as 1) getting psyched, 2) doing it, and 3) being in flow.

Simply by being aware of each of these steps in the execution phase, you will enhance your ability to overcome your fears, stop forcing your performance, and enjoy the process and experience of implementing your plans. Getting psyched is all about overcoming the little voice inside your head that attempts to implant negative thoughts and doubts. The second step is the moment when you initiate or execute your performance— the point of no return! This is the moment in which intention moves into action and you begin your performance. Once you have set the wheels in motion, flowing with the process is the last step. Have you ever experienced being fully engrossed in the task at hand and feeling both highly energized and extremely focused? That is what is called "flow." I believe that we will experience a state of flow whenever we have three things: clearly established goals; a solid level of mastery or competency in the activity—usually through lots of practice; achieved a balance between the level of challenge the activity presents and our present skills. Once you can master these three skills, you'll achieve a greater sense of satisfaction, both personally and professionally.

The execution phase is about realizing your fears and overcoming them in order to direct all of your energy into your performance and performing that with a complete, conscious enjoyment of the moment. This is the most exciting phase because it is about taking direct action towards goal attainment.

Assessment

The third phase in the *Winning Process* is assessment. Do you consistently sit down after a speech, sales call, meeting, or race, for example, and figure out what you did that was good versus what aspects of your performance could stand to be improved upon? If you haven't taken the time for a formal process of self-evaluation, then you're not alone. What I have found, time and again, is that people don't spend nearly enough time assessing their performance.

Assessment serves to reduce your preparation time, helps you to understand where to focus your future preparation time and, most importantly, it contributes to improved results.

Assessment serves to reduce your preparation time, helps you to understand where to focus your future preparation time and, most importantly, it contributes to improved results.

The important thing to remember when we're assessing our performance is that we all have our own biases and beliefs that affect how we undertake that self-assessment. That's natural, after all, not every activity can be measured with a stopwatch. Having said that, I will demonstrate the value of mastering the practice of stepping outside yourself, and trying to become more objective in your self-evaluations.

When you do take the time to assess your performance, do you look at the smallest factors or do you take a larger, big-picture view of your performance? I will tell you that it is sometimes the smallest factors that have the greatest impact on your performance and the end result. In fact, it's often more effective to break the whole into a series of smaller parts.

Identifying and assessing the factors that contribute to your performance will help you focus on the future, learn what is and is not working, and what you can and cannot control.

Identifying and assessing the factors that contribute to your performance will help you focus on the future, learn what is and is not working, and what you can and cannot control.

Rejuvenation

The final stage in the winning process is rejuvenation. While we all know the importance of taking a vacation, of spending time with our families, or just taking a short time-out when things get down to the wire and we're in a time crunch, rejuvenation is often the first thing to be pitched out the window. In the rush of day-to-day living and the struggle to succeed, taking time to relax often loses its importance. What working parent has time to get a massage? What busy executive or business owner has time to take a vacation?

Throughout my career as a professional skier, I was aware of the value of rejuvenation but it wasn't until much later in my life that I actually acted on my awareness and put the theory into practice. Real practice. Post World Cup circuit, I made rejuvenation a priority and can tell you that it has made a significant difference in my life. Currently, I take a minimum of 6 weeks off per year. In hindsight, I know that had I taken more time off while I was ski racing, it would have led to more victories. That's why I remind myself daily that taking time for rejuvenation is not only essential for my happiness and well-being, it has a direct influence on the level of success I can achieve. It makes success a sustainable outcome rather than just a destination.

> *Taking time for rejuvenation is not only essential for my happiness and well-being, it has a direct influence on the level of success I can achieve.*

Rejuvenation is vital to the process of success. Learn and implement this step and you will not only have better health, balance, and perspective, you will have increased effectiveness and focus, and more sustainable results. It took a major event to drill this lesson into my life practice.

The stories in this section all relate to how an adherence to this process can have a significant, positive impact on success. As you read through the four stories in this section, I invite you to take an honest look at your life, your goals, and the strategies that you're currently using to achieve your dreams. I encourage you to answer the questions and challenges that I pose at the end of each story and to incorporate the *Winning Process* in your daily life. Here's to winning and to living a winning life!

1.1

The Greatest Skill Athletes Can Teach You

If You Can See It, You Will Achieve It

"Close your eyes," the coach said, interrupting our post-practice basketball game. His voice echoed off the gymnasium walls. "Visualize the upcoming downhill course at Whistler." We formed a line across the gym and I closed my eyes. I pictured myself at the start gate. "Ten, nine, eight," coach counted down. "Four, three, two, one, go!"

Standing in the gym in my tennis shoes, surrounded by my teammates with my eyes closed, I pushed off from the starting gate. I got into my tuck position and I zipped down the course. I saw the turns, bumps, and gates and I maneuvered them expertly. I crossed the finish line and stood up. Opening my eyes, I saw I was the only one standing. Fifteen seconds later, another teammate stood, ten seconds later another, until finally the entire team had completed the visualization exercise.

"Cary," Coach said, looking at his stopwatch, "during that exercise you finished a course that takes 1 minute and 57 seconds, in 1 minute and 20 seconds. You're nowhere near real time." Turning to my teammate Rob Boyd, he said, "You hit it exactly on. Good job."

My coach had told me on various occasions how visualization would help me improve my performance. "Ya, ya," I'd thought, "I visualize all the time. I know how to do it." This exercise showed me that, perhaps, I wasn't so good at it after all.

Rob, on the other hand, appeared to be really good at visualization. At that time, he was also the only member on our team to have won a World Cup Downhill race. Perhaps his ability in visualization was connected to his winning performance?

After asking for his help, Rob had one key insight for me that made a huge difference. His insight was that he engaged all five senses during his visualization. He smelled the cedar at the starting gate. He felt the cold air on his skin and lips as he moved down the course. He heard the snow swooshing under his skis and the audience cheering. He pictured the audience cheering on the sidelines. He tasted the sticky saliva of excitement in his mouth.

Wow, I thought. All I'd been doing was visualizing the course, literally seeing myself skiing down the hill. I decided to practice my visualization exercises using Rob's technique. I grabbed a stopwatch and closed my eyes. I smelled the cedar at the starting gate; I heard the cheers from fans along the sidelines; I heard the countdown and tasted sunscreen and lipbalm in my mouth. I saw the course as I heard the official yell, 'GO!' and I felt the snow under my skis as I pushed off.

My visualizations became more exacting the more I practiced. My timing improved as did my sensory awareness. That year, after relentlessly practicing better visualization, I moved from 60th in the world rankings to 25th. I won two US Championships and placed 4th in the World Cup event held at Whistler, a result that bested my great teammate Rob Boyd on that occasion. I had harnessed the power of visualization!

As my skills in visualization improved, my confidence rose. I had underestimated the value and power of mental rehearsal. Every day you hear people rave about the benefits of visualization, but do you practice it? Do you really engage yourself in the process of visualization? I hadn't and I'd paid the price in progressing more slowly.

Now I know that if I can't see it and believe it, I probably will not achieve it. However, if I visualize whatever my goal happens to be, as if it were real and tangible, then my rate of success accelerates and I achieve my goals in a shorter period of time. I know exactly what it feels like to execute a stellar performance and exactly what it feels like to win.

> *Without visualizing the process by which we plan to achieve our goals, we'll have a more difficult time understanding what the journey to success looks or feels like.*

Visualization is not just a skill for athletes to use. I have used this technique to visualize everything from a great public presentation to a successful meeting with a business partner. The process helps raise our confidence, and I know it makes a difference to our performance execution.

Without visualizing the process by which we plan to achieve our goals, we'll have a more difficult time understanding what the journey to success looks or feels like. Without a clear plan, which we can see ourselves executing, we'll end up, at best, with a fuzzy focus, fuzzy execution, and fuzzy results. If we accurately visualize our goals and the steps to get there, we are less reactive during the actual implementation. We can be more proactive, more confident, and execute our performance with greater precision.

I wonder if you've ever tried to harness the power of visualization? I encourage you to visualize yourself engaging all five of your senses to achieve the perfect execution. Do you see yourself crossing the finish line and achieving your desired outcome or result?

I invite you to take just one minute each and every morning to visualize actually achieving a goal that you wish to accomplish. Practice and repetition make all the difference!

Notes To Yourself

_____

_____

_____

_____

_____

_____

_____

_____

_____

_____

_____

_____

_____

_____

_____

_____

_____

_____

_____

_____

_____

_____

_____

_____

_____

1.2

What Are You Doing Right?

How Focusing On Your Strengths Will Help You Succeed

Newspaper and television reporters surrounded me. Lights flashed, microphones buzzed. "You came in second," a reporter said, pointing his microphone in my direction. "Doesn't it make you mad to come in second again? Aren't you discouraged by losing the top podium in the World Cup Downhill Championships by just three one-hundredths of a second?"

"Yes," I admitted. "I am disappointed." I was happy to be on the World Cup podium for the second time but winning first place would have been great. "I am also encouraged," I told them.

"What do you mean?" the reporter asked, clearly confused by my optimism.

"I made some mistakes today," I said. "But I also know that I did a lot of things right. I know that I can correct the mistakes I made today and improve my run tomorrow."

You see, I had learned a lesson, years before, when I was at the US National Championships in Winter Park, Colorado. I learned the importance of focusing on both my strengths and my weaknesses to build on what I had done well as opposed to undermining my own confidence by excessively focusing on what I had failed to achieve.

During that previous race in Colorado, I placed first during the final training run, despite making a few mistakes. That evening, I spent several hours visualizing my errors and watching the videotape so that I could bring to awareness and then work to eliminate all of my errors on my performance the next day.

The following day, I absolutely nailed those aspects of my performance where I had made errors the day before, but I also totally blew different aspects of my performance and sections of the course

> *Maybe our emphasis on problems exists because focusing on fixing what is wrong feels like the "real work," whereas focusing on strengths (dare I say celebrating strengths) feels fluffy and not worthy of our time.*

which I had previously done well. Crossing the finish line, knowing that I had no hope of winning the race, I immediately realized what had happened.

You see, the night before, I had focused my attention only on learning what I had done wrong. By not crystallizing the things I had done well, I actually stopped doing them. As a consequence of this realization, I made a deliberate decision to hereafter always focus on my strengths as well as my weaknesses whenever I assessed my performance.

Why is it so easy for us to focus on what's wrong? Perhaps that mindset comes from our Western society that encourages "critical" thinking and emphasizes problem solving. Maybe our emphasis on problems exists because focusing on fixing what is wrong feels like the "real work," whereas focusing on strengths (dare I say celebrating strengths) feels fluffy and not worthy of our time. Regardless, this problem-based paradigm is a hard one to move away from—it is so pervasive.

As easy as it is to slip into old habits of focusing on improving our areas of weakness, the risk is that we cannot fully optimize our performances unless we're equally as conscious of what we're doing well. Recognizing both our strengths and our weaknesses will help us to achieve success more rapidly.

None of us are immune to this phenomenon. When we focus only on what we are doing wrong, we skew our perspective of our talent and we limit our ability to take our performance to the next level. Worse than this, we rob ourselves of the opportunity to feel great about ourselves along the way.

> *Recognizing both our strengths and our weaknesses will help us to achieve success more rapidly.*

Oh...you might be wondering what happened after I won second place in the World Cup Downhill. Well, that evening, I spent half my time focusing on my mistakes and the other half of the evening recognizing what I had done correctly, concentrating on how I could build upon the successes of the day's run. The next day, I won first place in the race by a mere five one-hundredths of a second. (And the press conference, this time around, was much more fun!)

I ask you, is this tendency we have for focusing on our flaws showing up in your life, and how? Are you ignoring your strengths? When was the last time that you really recognized your successes so that you could repeat them? I invite you to take the time to not only work on your weaknesses—that is the easy part—but to also spend the same amount of time recognizing what you do well.

Notes To Yourself

_____

_____

_____

_____

_____

_____

_____

_____

_____

_____

_____

_____

_____

_____

_____

_____

_____

_____

_____

_____

_____

_____

_____

_____

_____

_____

_____

_____

1.3

The Falldown Plan

With A "Plan B" In Motion You Can Accelerate Your Results

At the end of a particularly frustrating ski season I opened my diary in search of clues to explain why I'd fallen short of achieving my goals. After rereading the notes I'd made after about 50 races that season, it became apparent I had a significant recurring problem. Day in and day out I had written, "I was too tight today. I just didn't relax sufficiently or perform as well as in training."

I've always been a big advocate of positive thinking and I'd been trying the mantras and the breathing exercises but clearly this still hadn't been enough. After reading the same thing over and over again in my diary, I realized I would have to be honest with myself and try and answer to myself why, deep down " I felt so stressed out? Why am I so tight?" I finally realized it was because I felt my whole life and future was riding on one outcome—winning a World Cup race or an Olympic medal. Since the age of six I had been single-mindedly focused on becoming the best downhill skier in the world. Deep down I worried about the possibility of walking away from the sport—at the age 26 or 28—with nothing more than some great travel experiences and a large number of frequent flier points.

I'd witnessed teammates on the National ski teams retire and enter the world of work after skiing with varying degrees of success; some had excelled in their chosen pursuits and others had not done so well at all. I realized that I was worried about having no money when it came time for me to retire from the ski circuit. I could've spent this same time and effort on earning an MBA or PhD or some other more valuable employment experience.

That's what I was stressed about—I had it all riding on a pair of Atomics!

For most people, the two enduring truths in ski racing are that eventually you'll either be replaced by a faster horse or you'll retire injured.

I was an aggressive skier and although I was optimistic I wouldn't get injured, in an effort to try and alleviate the excessive pressure I was placing upon myself, I decided to go beyond the mantras and breathing exercises. I needed to address the root cause of my stress rather than just the symptoms. I determined that I needed to start planning an exit strategy for myself, which would include some sort of financial safety net.

What I needed was a fall back plan, maybe even a "falldown" plan, if I should be injured, so that whenever the next stage of my life after skiing actually began, then I would have a financial nest egg to help me initiate the next stage of my life.

This realization and thinking was what actually got me started pursuing opportunities in real estate—something with which I'd been fascinated by for years.

Both my parents were teaching school full time but they were also entrepreneurs on the side.

When we lived in Calgary, my father and my grandpa purchased some land that they eventually planned on selling to real estate developers as the city expanded.

After flipping that property, my father parlayed the proceeds into an 18-suite apartment building in Banff, Alberta where I was first exposed to the business in undertaking everything from fielding phone calls, to vacuuming corridors and lobbies, painting and decorating, and renting out suites.

At about the age of 19, my father gave me a book on real estate by Robert Allen called *Creating Wealth* which had a considerable impact on my life. I was really quite infatuated by it all and I wanted to act on what I had learned but didn't do so until much later.

At the age of 20, I took the course to gain my real estate salesperson's license. I took the course simply to gain more knowledge from an investment standpoint. At the age of 21 I purchased my first house in a rather remote community that had been projected to experience an economic boom: Prince George, British Columbia. It was a bold investment play and when Prince George became the fastest growing city in Canada I doubled my real estate investment within a year.

Following this, I purchased four properties in Banff, and subsequently more than doubled my investment on each of them. Thereafter, I kept flipping properties to reach the point where I now own 60 units in the oil-rich province of Alberta alone.

> *Having the (fall back or fall down) plan in place helped remove a significant amount of pressure. I found I could relax and experienced a much-improved ability to perform to my potential.*

Whether it's condo conversions, residential rentals or real estate development, having a career in real estate has remained a significant passion.

Going back to my ski-racing career, my realization that I needed to develop a "fall down" plan actually allowed me to breathe and relax when ski-racing. Having the plan in place helped remove a significant amount of pressure. I found I could relax and experienced a much-improved ability to perform to my potential.

Ultimately, my "fall down" plan helped me to find my zone and both relax and enjoy my ski racing to become a World Cup champion and world downhill speed record holder in Kitzbuhel, Austria.

I urge you to assess yourself. Is there an aspect or part of your life where you are overly stressed? Ask yourself deep down, "What's causing this stress?"

Then undertake more than the positive thinking: address it and build a plan for yourself that helps you enjoy the process. Find your flow for greater results. Heck, it might urge you to get on and do something that you should have done anyway. I'm eternally grateful that the stress I experienced urged me to invest early. Having done this, I'm now able to embark on my latest venture that involves building a beachfront resort years earlier than ever I dreamed. It's my dream to create a place for family and friends to come and enjoy the sun, one another and their lives. I wish you the best in fulfilling your own dreams. Assess what's preventing you from achieving greater results, then address the cause and develop a plan of action. Then follow your plan.

If you'd like to take a look at my resort in Mexico, please visit **www.VivoResorts.com**.

Notes To Yourself

1.4

Do Sweat The Small Stuff

Lessons From A Wind Tunnel In Buffalo

You should have seen me storming around that day. I was like an angry bull, kicking at the ground and knocking things out of my way. And just like an angry bull, there was no reasoning with me.

You see, I had left the lodgings that morning convinced I was one of the fastest racers on the ski team. Only a few hours later, I discovered that I was actually the slowest. Not second slowest, or third, but bottom of the heap. And the worst part about it was that I didn't have a clue as to why.

We were in Buffalo that day using one of the same wind tunnels that NASA uses to test prototype rockets. That's one of the perks of being a ski racer—hanging out in wind tunnels. Anyway, the idea is that wind tunnel testing can be used to improve your aerodynamics which, in turn, serves to improve your race time. In ski racing, every one-hundredth of a second is critical. The team was there that day so that each of us could work on our tuck position—that's the position skiers take when they're on a flat or straight section of the course and they want to build up as much speed as possible.

I learned a great deal that day. Not just about tuck positions either. The testing schedule provided each team member with a number of turns in the tunnel, whereupon we would adopt our tuck position and obtain a wind resistance reading. The lower the resistance, the faster your tuck position would be. In my case, I should say, the higher the resistance, the slower you would be.

After the first go-round, my resistance reading placed me as the slowest. I didn't make a big deal of it. "No problem," I thought, "I just need to fix my tuck." For my second trial, I adopted a lower tuck position and I held my arms in a different position. I came in last again! "That's OK, I'll get there in the end," I told myself. I hadn't yet let my poor performance get under my skin. I prepared for my third trial holding my legs closely together and stretched my arms to place my hands as far in front of me as I could manage. Again, the tortoise of the team! Subsequently, trials went from bad to worse all morning. No matter how I modified my position, I kept coming in last. I can't tell you how frustrated I was feeling. Well, actually I can—*very* frustrated, and exceedingly embarrassed to boot! It was around the 4th trial that the bewildered muttering began. By round 6, I was stamping my feet. By round eight, I was throwing my gloves around and growling out the kind of colorful language that would be the hallmark of a Quentin Tarantino movie!

What the heck was going on? Nothing made any sense to me. At 210 lbs—by no means the lightest person on the squad—I was coming in behind teammates who were heavier-set than me by 40 lbs or better? Surely bigger guys create more wind-resistance? My performance seemed at odds with the basic laws of physics!

By the time I was into my tenth trial, I had tried every position I could think of and yet my resistance ratings continued to put me in last place. To be honest, I was getting a bit desperate. So, I took a deep breath and told myself, "look, I can't be the slowest one here, there has to be something else I can do." And I started going through every possible factor, one by one, no matter how irrelevant or trivial they sounded. If it wasn't my tuck position, what could it be?

Perhaps the solution lay with some aspect of my equipment? I took a look at my ski poles, goggles, and helmet. There wasn't much I could change there—the other guys all used pretty much the same gear. I guessed I could change my helmet and try one of an alternate design with a smaller wind flap and a slightly lower back. But, realistically how much difference would that make, I thought?

Nevertheless, I decided I had nothing left to lose. I tried on the new helmet. I took my next turn and the resistance reading I achieved shot me up to the middle of the rankings. Combining the new helmet with a new arm position, holding my hands way forward, I rose to the top of the rankings and achieved the lowest resistance score of the morning.

It was a great feeling. Not only was I now the fastest member of the team, I had solved a problem that I had thought was beyond redemption. All morning, I'd been flailing around

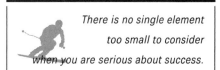

There is no single element too small to consider when you are serious about success.

searching for the answer to explain my high resistance readings. Now that I'd found it, I realized it had been on my head the whole time.

In hindsight, it's clear I shouldn't have assumed that my first choice of helmet was the best choice. I'd heard that the model had done well in wind tunnel tests and that had been good enough for me. But I should have revisited that assumption earlier in the trials instead of just ruling it out as a potential performance factor.

The way I had been thinking that day, I simply didn't have time to worry about equipment. I was too busy working on the bigger picture— on my technique, my tuck position, my fitness, my weightlifting, and my exact intake of carbohydrates and proteins. I was so absorbed with calculating my caloric intake to the nearest cracker, I was blind to other factors that were so much more basic.

Admittedly, my attitude to coming last all the time wasn't exactly helpful. I was so annoyed and embarrassed: the feelings had clouded my vision. The more I failed to obtain a good result, the more stressed I became. If I hadn't become so rattled by my poor results, I might have stopped to reconsider my equipment a little earlier.

Instead, I took my equipment for granted. I just assumed that if the equipment worked for other people, then it would work for me. The thought of trying a different helmet didn't even enter my mind.

That day in the wind tunnel taught me that there is no single element too small to consider when you are serious about success. You can become so caught up in searching through all of the big factors, when sometimes, all along, it's the little things that end up being the source of the problem and, once fixed, make a huge difference.

I realized that I needed to identify and consider the little things as well. Details are important! I can't just assume that if something works for other people, then it will work for me too—I need to test it for myself.

I also realized that perseverance in and with the winning process eventually led me to the answer—however infuriating it was! If I hadn't kept at it in the wind tunnel that day, I would never have learned that I needed a new helmet. It's crucial to receive constant feedback. After all, to win we need the best resources, the best techniques, the best technology, and the best equipment.

I wonder if there are any "small" or "basic" factors in your life that you are taking for granted?

In what areas are you handicapping yourself by not working with optimal equipment and technology? Could your personal approach to conducting business—your attitude, demeanor, and communication skills—benefit from a review and some fine tuning? It could be something as small as uttering a single sentence in which you ask your client for the business at the end of your meeting. Have you really tested all of your success factors to see how they work for you in particular, or have you accepted cookie-cutter solutions in accepting whatever other people have told you works for them?

What are the factors that may be impacting your performance that you haven't yet taken time to seriously consider? For those of you who work directly with people, you may be surprised to learn that our communication techniques are the single most overlooked success factor for most people. There are a myriad of skills and practices that impact how effective and compelling we are in our communication with others.

Make sure you take care of the little things. Don't just look for the grand solutions. Fine-tune your performance for greater success and seek out the resources that can carry you to a higher level of performance and success.

1.5

Knock Some Sense Into Your Head!

The Lost Art Of Rejuvenation

I felt a wave of delicious, wonderful energy flowing back into me…more energy than I remembered having in years. Lying on the couch, recovering from a concussion, it felt like energy was flowing into me instead of draining out of me.

As I lay on the couch, I realized that I had not taken a real vacation in seventeen years. After all those years of working 80-hour weeks without a break, now, as fate would have it, I was being forced to take time off. I suddenly realized how big a mistake I had made.

Being an athlete, I had been taught the value of rejuvenation by many of my predecessors, some of them leading performers in my sport. I recall that Tommy Moe took a week off just before the Olympic Games in Norway and he won the Gold Medal. Similarly, the year that Kyle Rasmussen took a week off before the World Cup, he came in first. Danny Maher, who held the record for the longest, continuous tenure on the World Cup circuit (16 years), routinely took six weeks off each spring after the racing season had ended.

Knowing the value of rejuvenation and practicing it were two different things. For much of my skiing career, I was simply too afraid to take time off. Even in the spring when the competition was over, I'd jump right into my off-season training schedule—lifting weights and doing whatever I thought I needed to do to get ahead of the game for the following season. I did this year after year despite chronic patella tendonitis arising from not taking sufficient downtime to allow my muscles and joints to recuperate.

Now that I was being forced to take time off, I was experiencing the value of downtime firsthand. All my life, I've had a tendency to push and extend myself, sometimes relentlessly so. While I believe that this ability is one of my greatest strengths, it is also one of my greatest weaknesses. Lying on the couch, I committed myself to making a formal plan for taking time off on a regular basis.

Years later, as an entrepreneur and business owner, I was faced with that familiar feeling of being afraid to take time off. I was worried about not being around to make important business decisions and that my competition would get ahead of me in my absence. I was allowing short-term fear to dictate my decision making instead of focusing on the amazing long-term possibilities of what could happen if I were to integrate periods of time for rejuvenation into my life.

One morning, I realized that I was getting caught up in my unrelenting cycle of work again, just as I had when I was ski racing. To counteract the pattern, I immediately scheduled three weeks of vacation on my calendar. I marked the dates in ink on our kitchen calendar. I committed myself to the plan of adding a further week each year until I had booked off six weeks of annual vacation time.

> The truth is, if we don't take time off to re-energize, we fall into bad habits. We get drained of our energy and enthusiasm; we lose our perspective and our creativity.

That first year, I took three weeks of vacation. I made no business-related phone calls, and neither wrote nor answered any business-related email. I did nothing. I spent the time in Maui with my family simply relaxing and having fun. The experience was amazing! I returned home and to work with energy and a renewed sense of creativity and excitement for my business and my life.

I've continued with this plan and I've watched my success grow. Since implementing the rejuvenation plan, I have been voted one of the 26 hottest speakers of the year by *Successful Meetings* magazine and I am on track to achieve both my financial and personal goals. All of these business achievements have happened while I continue to take six weeks off each year, which I spend with my family at our beach house in Puerto Escondido, Mexico. Despite how hard I work and how busy I am, I have built a sustainable success model around taking time off and rejuvenating.

The truth is, if we don't take time off to re-energize, we fall into bad habits. We get drained of our energy and enthusiasm; we lose our perspective and our creativity. Rejuvenation is different for everyone. It could be a pattern of activities that focus on physical rest, gentle exercise, undertaking a cleanse or detoxification diet, spa treatments, a retreat or period of meditation, or even time to indulge in your favorite sport or pastime. The main thing is to discover what is rejuvenating for you and to do that activity on a regular basis. Do you see yourself embroiled in a non-stop pattern of work? Are you taking enough time off to rejuvenate? It doesn't have to be three weeks. It can be as simple as a weekly massage or taking time each day to read a good book. What is rejuvenating for you? Once you know what re-energizes you, make it a priority, schedule the time off, and book it into your calendar of commitments with equal priority to the other important business meetings and commitments!

Notes To Yourself

_____

_____

_____

_____

_____

_____

_____

_____

_____

_____

_____

_____

_____

_____

_____

_____

_____

_____

_____

_____

_____

_____

_____

_____

_____

_____

_____

2
Pick Your Line

S UCCESS IS HOWEVER YOU CHOOSE TO DEFINE IT. What are your goals? How do you define achievement?

Picking your line simply means that you establish your goal, any goal, and you focus on achieving it. If I were to ask you to define your goals, would you be able to answer me? What if I asked about your plan to achieve your goals...would you have a clear road map for goal attainment to share with me?

As children we're allowed to dream, but as we grow into adults we often neglect our power to dream. We deny ourselves permission to dream because we've been taught to focus on all of the barriers that might prevent us from achieving our goals. I want you to reinvigorate your power to dream! I want you to realize that there are endless possibilities and I want you to allow yourself to dream without restrictions.

- *What do you really want to do?*
- *What do you want to have?*
- *Who do you want to become?*

Did you know that we often achieve our best results when we're happy and that we're happiest when we're striving for clearly established goals?

In this section we will address the importance of goals—both goal setting and goal achievement. There are so many factors that can take us off track and cause us to lose our focus and take our attention away from our intended goals. It happens to everyone and it happens to me in the course of daily living.

When you pick your line, or identify your goal, you must keep your goal at the forefront of your mind every day. Each day, from the time you wake up until you go to sleep at night, you need to have clarity of purpose. With a clear goal in mind, you will be able to achieve your goals more quickly, and with greater precision.

> Did you know that we often achieve our best results when we're happy and that we're happiest when we're striving for clearly established goals?

Conducting your life by setting measurable, attainable goals that you can direct all of your focus and attention towards is a secret that elite athletes have internalized and integrated so that it is an inherent aspect of their daily practice. From short-term goals, such as, "I want to do 100 sit-ups," to our longer-term goals, such as, "I want to win a World Cup," we know our actions have an ultimate purpose.

Your goals may be different. I want to lose ten pounds. I want to buy the house I've had my eye on in that elite neighborhood. I want to be the top salesperson in my company. I want my business to gross $500,000 this year. Whatever your goal may be, in whatever field you are in, this secret works.

Picking your line means making a choice not to do a lot of other things; it allows you to confirm your motivation and sharpen your focus on your own goals, and do so for your own reasons. By picking your line, you will realize the power of focus. Take a moment at the end of each of the following stories, to reflect on your own life.

Here are 5 strategies to consider as you "Pick your line":

1) Sometimes we need to make a difficult decision and choose between two desirable outcomes. That means dropping something.
2) Being strategic and playing to your strengths is a critical part of picking your line. We want to channel our efforts where we have the best chance of succeeding. Look long term too.
3) Be passionate. If we're not passionate then it's not a winning path. Not following your passion has negative impacts on our energy levels and on our health and over all well-being.
4) Make sure your goals are your own. Be clear that your goals are not merely externally driven and are actually someone else's, like our spouse, parents or coaches.

5) Goals and picking your line is about personal growth and becoming your best. Resist the temptation to think that it's ALL about results.

How can you find focus? How can you embrace this secret in order to live a winning life?

> Picking your line means making a choice not to do a lot of other things; it allows you to confirm your motivation and sharpen your focus on your own goals, and do so for your own reasons.

Read on and I'll show you how to tap into your clarity and passion so that you can achieve better results. As you read I challenge you to take a hard look at the goals you have set for yourself and answer the questions posed at the end of each story. I encourage you to learn how to stop settling for anything less than you deserve and begin receiving more of what you actually want!

Notes To Yourself

2.1

Put All Your Eggs In One Basket

Stop Dividing Your Focus And Start Winning

Following a presentation I made last week, a female member of the audience stayed behind to ask me a question. "Cary, you seemed to know that you would be a professional skier from such an early age, but you also said that you were largely unsuccessful at this sport for most of your youth. How were you able to stay so dedicated to a sport in which you experienced significant struggles during those early years? I mean, how did you find a way not to give up ski racing to try something else where you might have experienced success more quickly?"

While she was right about my dedication to skiing, I had not shared with her, or with that particular audience, that I had "cheated on" or in fact deviated from my skiing career. It all started out innocently enough, when I was about 10 years old. At that time, I started gymnastics with a view to improving my skiing performance. Within two years, I had moved to the United States for twelve months of study and training at a gymnastics academy in Eugene, Oregon. It was during this year of training that my dabbling in gymnastics turned into a more serious commitment to the sport.

After attending the academy, my performance ability in gymnastics soared, significantly out-performing my results in ski racing over a very short period of time. As a gymnast, I became a provincial champion, then a regional champion, and finally a national champion. As a ski racer, I was still completely unranked, and rarely won races despite my efforts to do so. I began to fantasize about being a world champion gymnast, thinking, "Maybe this is the sport at which I'm meant to be the best in the world." I became increasingly infatuated with gymnastics as it brought me the experience I most craved— winning! I was still reluctant to give up my true love, skiing, which

41

had been my sole passion for so many years. I decided that I would simply pursue both sports.

Initially, competing in both sports was fine, but I naively believed my ski racing wouldn't be affected by my divided attention. Indeed, I firmly believed I had the potential to become a champion in both sports. Participating in both gymnastics and ski racing required some skillful maneuvering, time management, and no small amount of compromise, but I figured the double duty effort was all worth it. By the time I was 15 years old, I was living in Calgary, away from my immediate family, so that I could ski race on the weekends and train in gymnastics during the week. I was competing nationally in both sports simultaneously. I didn't believe I needed to choose one sport over the other—at fifteen, I thought I could have it all.

For a few years, I was quite adept in juggling both sports, dividing my time, energy, and passion more or less equally. Eventually, the double duty took its toll, and my world started to crumble. Without a full-time focus on skiing, my race results steadily declined over a period of two years. In pursuing both sports, I had rationalized and accepted that my skiing performance might suffer a bit, yet I couldn't avoid the fact that my gymnastic results were also starting to slide, albeit ever so slightly. In trying to compete in both sports, neither one was receiving the attention or focus it warranted. I felt horrible. I knew that both sports deserved more than I was currently giving either of them, and yet I was also afraid to give up either one of them.

I hedged my bets. By keeping one foot in each sport, I felt I was giving myself two chances to 'make it'. The thought of reducing my chances to just one activity and one arena in which to win was frightening; I had been juggling both sports for too long to easily let go. I was also concerned about letting either of my coaches down, which I felt I would be doing if I let go of either sport. I wanted to avoid the tough conversation I imagined would take place in discussing 'breaking up' with either of them. How could I disappoint them after all the time and energy they had invested in me, never mind the time and energy I had invested in both pursuits?

Truth be told, I was already letting my coaches down. My divided focus was getting in the way of my living up to my full potential in either sport. I realized if I continued to try and focus on both gymnastics and ski racing, I was unlikely to be a champion in either sport. Instead, I would likely end up being mediocre in both. In attempting to have it all, I was more likely to end up with nothing,

> *If you study the most successful individuals in the world, from virtually any field you choose, you will find they have focused on one thing and one thing only.*

and certainly not the kind of results I was aiming for. I knew that I needed to commit to one sport exclusively. I was absolutely torn between the two and felt utterly stymied. Which sport was the right one for me? I had experienced such immediate results from gymnastics and was still struggling to achieve any similar results in ski racing. Should I give up skiing? I had invested so much time in ski racing. It seemed impossible to determine what was the right thing to do.

As I reflect on this difficult decision today, twenty years later, I realize that many of my most difficult life and career decisions have been similar to this early experience. Picking between something that is so clearly good and something that is not is a great deal easier than deciding the best option between two seemingly great opportunities. For example, recently I had to choose whether to remain with an organization and hope to receive a promotion, or strike out on my own and become an entrepreneur. My wife and I were also discussing whether we would try to have a third child or focus our time and energy on the two children we already had (both under three years old) and put our remaining time and energy into other aspects of our home and family life. Both situations required a decision, and yet it seemed there was no single right decision. Indecision is absolutely paralyzing in such situations.

As you know, I did end up picking skiing over gymnastics and I am completely convinced that it was the right decision. How I was able to arrive at that decision is another story (one that I share next in Stop Wasting Time and Start Chasing the Right Dream.) Ultimately, I was able to resolve the dilemma of which sport to pursue by lunging forward and simply making a decision. Once we have identified our fears, the next step is to make a decision, and lunge forward. I now realize how important it is to choose a direction—pick a line—and focus all of our

> *When we split or divide our focus, it becomes virtually impossible to obtain the same results we are capable of achieving when we have a single focus.*

effort and commit 100%. I know that the common advice is "Don't put all of your eggs in one basket." Yet, if you study the most successful individuals in the world, from virtually any field you choose, you will find they have focused on one thing and one thing only. Until I identified what was to become that one thing for myself, I was dividing my efforts and my energy. Initially, cross training strengthened my ability in both sports. Over time however, it undermined my potential in both. In putting less than 100% of myself—time, energy, passion and commitment—towards each sport, my results in both suffered. When we split or divide our focus, it becomes virtually impossible to obtain the same results we are capable of achieving when we have a single focus.

Take some time to think about your present life circumstances and whether your current level of success is suffering because of a lack of focus? Are you experiencing a dilemma of choice and avoiding the need to make a decision and a clear commitment to something that could take your success to the next level? In what areas have you divided your attention and your effort? Where are you playing to short-term results rather than looking at the long-term? What do you need to let go of so that you can direct more of your efforts towards a single focus?

2.2

Stop Wasting Time And Start Chasing The Right Dream

How To Move From Indecision To Clarity

When I was 15 years old, I recall a conversation I had with my father about which of the two sports—gymnastics and ski-racing—I should pursue exclusively and, of the two, in which arena I stood the most chance of becoming the best in the world. I'm getting a bit ahead of myself, so let me describe what led up to our discussion that night.

When I was 10 years old, I began cross training in gymnastics with the view to improving my ski racing performance. By the time I was 15, I was seriously competing in both gymnastics and ski racing simultaneously. It didn't take long before my performance in both sports began to decline. My split focus was preventing me from living up to my potential in either sport.

I knew that I needed to commit to one sport exclusively, but which one? At the time, I was a national champion in gymnastics and still struggling to achieve any similar result in ski racing. It was tempting to go with where I was winning, but I had invested a significant amount of time in ski racing; it was impossible for me, at 15, to let go of it altogether. I was also deeply afraid to give up either sport for fear I would subsequently discover I had given up the wrong one. I had two huge opportunities in front of me and no clear way of knowing where to focus my time, energy, passion, and commitment. I felt confused and utterly lost. It seemed impossible to know what was the right thing to do.

I turned to my father for guidance. After listening to my dilemma, he found a blank sheet of paper and a pen and said, "Well Cary, it's pretty clear that you want to be the best in the world at something. You seem to have narrowed that down to sport. Is that a fair summary?" I nodded in agreement. Dad then said, "Let's decide which sport, gymnastics or ski racing, in which you stand the greatest chance of becoming the best in the world." Dad continued by asking, "Which sport do you enjoy the most?" This question brought me right to the crux of my dilemma: I actually enjoyed both sports tremendously. My dad responded, "Well, let's look more strategically at both sports, and try and determine where you stand the best chance of success."

On a single sheet of paper, we proceeded to explore both sports with the goal of identifying which one presented the best opportunities for my future success. Together we learned that Canada had never produced a gymnast who had bettered a ranking of 33rd in the world. In ski racing, however, Canada had a record of producing 7 world cup champion ski racers. We also had a pragmatic discussion about my physique and potential winning capacity in both sports. At 5' 1" and 93 pounds, I was small for a 15 year old. These physical attributes were a great advantage in a sport like gymnastics where power-to-weight ratio and body awareness are both critical to success. In fact, we found there has never been a world champion gymnast over 5' 8". On the other hand, my body build was a considerable disadvantage in ski racing because it is a gravity-based sport. If you roll a big rock and a small rock down the hill, the big rock gets to the bottom first. My dad said, "Let's look a little longer term, Cary. You'll be at the top of your game between the ages of 21 and 28. Look at your genetics. Every man in your family line, including me, is 6' tall and 200 pounds. It seems as though you might end up being somewhere around 6' tall and 200 pounds." If I ended up with a physique like that, I would be much more competitive as a ski-racer than a gymnast.

My father switched his focus, and asked me another critical question, "What do you want to walk away from sport with?" I said, "I want to be the best in the world." He smiled. "Cary, I know you want to win. What else do you need to take away from this experience?" I replied, "Besides recognition, I want to make enough money in the sport to give me a head start into whatever I choose to do afterwards."

We compared endorsements, sponsorships, and prize money in both gymnastics and ski racing. As a Canadian gymnast at the time, even if you were to become the best in the world, there appeared to be very little money to be made. In ski racing, however, the individuals who were among the best in the world were earning several hundreds of thousands to millions of dollars each year.

Critically review all of your strengths and determine your risk-to-reward ratio so that you can be confident in knowing where your best opportunity for success lies.

The outcome of our conversation that night was a decision that I would give up gymnastics. As I reflect on that evening, I am struck most by the fact that I had this conversation when I was just 15 years old. I wonder how many people have reaped the benefit of a similar mentoring experience and conversation, not necessarily with a parent, but with anyone else, at any time in their life, never mind at such an early age. I know that I need to continue to have many more conversations of this same type both to mentor others, including my own children, as well as to be mentored myself.

In thinking about this experience, I feel overwhelmed by how fortunate I was to have a father who was both present and possessed the skills to conduct such a conversation with me at such a critical time in my early life. He believed in my vision of becoming a world champion and unconditionally supported me in pursuing that vision. My father was forward-thinking and strategic in helping me to make the best decision by identifying my strengths and clarifying my risk-to-reward ratio. Even though I had experienced greater success in gymnastics, skiing looked like a more likely arena in which I could become a world champion over the longer term. The potential financial rewards in ski racing were also much more attractive. The decision process I worked through with my father helped me to be confident in the choice I was making. If I had not been able to determine where I might have the best opportunity for success, I would never have become a world champion; passion alone would not have been enough.

I wonder if you've had the good fortune to explore similar life and career questions for yourself. Are you in the right sport, in the right industry, in the right role? Do you know where your best chance of succeeding lies in the long-term? Are you able to articulate what it is you really wish to do, so that you become the best in the world? I encourage you to critically review all of your strengths and determine your risk-to-reward ratio so that you can be confident in knowing where your best opportunity for success lies.

Notes To Yourself

2.3

Alive With Vivo Resorts

Is Oceanfront Living Just A Dream? Your Power Of Decision

Several years ago, on one of my beach vacations to Maui, I made a very clear decision—someday I'm going to own a home on the ocean and, moving forward, I'm going to take time off to really enjoy it. It is interesting to me that when we make a definitive decision our mind starts to work on strategies and solutions for fulfilling the dream. Right there and then, I began a quest—to find what I thought would be the best beachfront property in the world for my desired lifestyle as well as for an investment. I wanted it to be a place where I was able to live and practice a healthy and balanced life and simply enjoy the present moment.

Over the interim years, I spent a significant amount of my spare time on research, via the internet, looking at real estate opportunities in more than 30 countries. Then I embarked on a rather ambitious schedule of public speaking events, in 13 countries around the world. In each location, I would always make time for a real estate tour to investigate oceanfront property.

Following my parents' retirement to Palm Springs, I took notice of what was and wasn't good about the region for us—their children—when we visited them during the winter. I began recognizing and developing a list of criteria which I felt were important in selecting a destination for a winter vacation or second home.

Over the years, my list of criteria has grown to 44 factors to consider before purchasing a retirement, recreation or investment property. My list includes everything from rainfall patterns and ocean temperatures, to the assessed potential for large real estate value appreciation.

It's a list anyone could apply to pretty much any real estate investment, although each one of us would rank the factors according to our own personal priorities. After all of this research, I concluded that Mexico was undervalued and the next place to boom both from a lifestyle as well as an investment perspective.

At one point, I was a handshake away from purchasing a large property near Villahermosa, Mexico (primarily because it was cheap). Fortunately for me, before the deal was sealed, I recalled the mistake I had made years before when I invested in property in Strathmore, Alberta as opposed to Canmore, Alberta. At the time, condos in Strathmore were going for about $40,000 as opposed to $60,000 in the more highly desirable recreational town of Canmore nestled in the Rocky Mountains. The Strathmore condos are now worth around $200,000, while the Canmore units are $600,000 each. Somehow, back then, I had justified the decision in my own mind that my purchase of the cheaper of the two made better business sense. Looking back, it is hindsight that enables me to say that properties in areas with greater recreational potential generally produce higher returns. The other significant advantage of a property investment with recreational destination potential is that the potential exists for you to use the property yourself to enhance your current lifestyle in the interim. Furthermore, it has the potential to become one of your best financial investments.

Learning from the mistake I made early on in my real estate career, I've come to realize that when investing in property, it's far more profitable to focus on what has the most potential and value over the long term, not merely on what is the cheapest in the present. For all my real estate investments, I also like to ask myself "what do I want to own for my personal use?"

After taking several trips through many of the coastal areas of Mexico, I finally found the right location in Puerto Escondido.

Puerto Escondido has the best of what remains of the real Mexico. A quietly vibrant surfing beach town and fishing village that the locals from Mexico City know about, Puerto Escondido boasts miles of pristine unspoiled beaches and warm, energizing turquoise water. I believe its undervalued real estate is going to skyrocket in value over the next decade.

Here's how Puerto Escondido stacked up regarding some of the 44 factors: on the tropical southern Pacific coast of Mexico, this small fishing, surfing and tourist town of about 50,000 people has a low risk of hurricanes, beautiful long beaches, less rainfall than Hawaii (0% in the winter time), and warmer ocean water than the Caribbean. Puerto Escondido has an international airport but presently there

> *When investing in property, it's far more profitable to focus on what has the most potential and value over the long term, not merely on what is the cheapest in the present.*

aren't many direct flights available. However, it is located just 100 km from another international airport that presently receives several flights each week from Canada, the US and the UK. Mexican President Calderon recently identified the Puerto Escondido area as "a new, truly international center of tourist development". The region has been touted by *Frommers Travel* as "the best overall beach value in Mexico," and *Conde Nast* also just placed it on their 2008 list of must visit places in the world. With a solid infrastructure in place and more plans in the works, more and more Mexicans and tourists from around the world are visiting Puerto Escondido's beautiful Emerald Coast where they discover some of the world's best weather, surfing, and real estate value.

On the basis of my own research as well as these international endorsements, I purchased a home in Puerto Escondido where we spend the bulk of our winters with family and friends. I've also purchased a beautiful parcel of oceanfront land that is currently under development and being transformed into VIVO Resorts.

VIVO Resorts is a brand new resort community being built from the ground up under my personal direction and vision for a full amenity destination based around life balance and healthy living. VIVO Resorts will shortly be the place to enjoy the best of your life for the rest of your life, starting now. I call it the world's first semi-retirement haven.

The 75-acre paradise resort will include 100 home sites and 375 condominiums and will feature everything from a spa and fitness centre, each with an ocean view, to a cutting edge business centre and infinity pools.

The development is located in what is, year round, a pleasantly warm, tropical environment where family and friends can come together and enjoy these amenities and activities with one another. I tried to find all this elsewhere, but I couldn't, so I had to develop it. It

> *Whether you are investing in people, products, services, or property, ask yourself whether you are buying the cheapest or what represents the best value?*

is a place to live on the beach and enjoy time with your favorite people.

There is no doubt that I love Canada. However, since I retired from ski racing, winters just aren't as much fun for me any more. What keeps me connected to Canada, at least for part of the year, are my roots, and these obviously include my family and friends.

My father has teased me for a long time over my quest to find the perfect warm-weather destination and just last year he admitted to me that he finally figured out why.

"It's because for all those years you were involved in ski racing, you spent 12 months a year chasing snow." According to my father, or so he likes to joke, in chasing winter across two hemispheres, I've lived almost as many winters as an 80-year-old man. Not any more!

As the resort is being built, I'm on site, working with my builders to ensure the vision I've been forming in my mind for years comes to fruition. Just as it was when I was ski racing, I might be the pilot but it takes a solid team behind you to achieve the type of success I know Vivo Resorts will eventually become.

I'm pleased I didn't make the same real estate mistake again and purchase where land and property were cheaper. I also didn't purchase where land and property were the most expensive either. This time I invested in the area I truly believed offered the best lifestyle and investment value, and where I also wanted to be, and where I wanted my family to be.

Whether you are investing in people, products, services, or property, ask yourself whether you are buying the cheapest or what represents the best value? Are your investments enhancing your life right now, or are you merely hoping they will someday?

If you have also "Picked Your Line" and have decided to live on the ocean, then I might have done the research for you. I invite you to review and consider our paradise and come and be my neighbor at VIVO Resorts. In care you are wondering, VIVO means "Alive".

Visit us at **www.VivoResorts.com** or contact me at **info@Vivo Resorts.com**.

2.4

Increase Your Success Factor

How Following Your Passion Can Improve Your Results

The room resonated with the familiar hum of the garage door opening. Turning off the television, I jumped from the couch and sprinted into the kitchen to set the stovetop timer for two minutes. Mom was home! Dashing back into the front room, I slid onto the bench next to my brother, who'd just opened the piano.

Just as we settled into our positions, the door opened. Mom walked into the house and smiled at her two children, apparently diligently working through their daily piano practice. Two minutes later, the timer went off. My brother and I closed the piano, announcing, "that's our 30 minutes of practice done," and headed outside to play.

This pattern of deceit went on for three years. You see, originally, I had wanted to play the piano. At six years old, I thought it would be cool to be a famous piano player. My parents were excited to expose us to as many things as possible, especially cultural activities, so they jumped at the opportunity to set up piano lessons. They believed, as I do, that you cannot find what you are passionate about without being exposed to a variety of experiences.

It didn't take many lessons, perhaps three or four, before I decided that I didn't really like playing the piano. My older brother felt the same way. When we both realized neither of us was really keen on piano lessons, we developed our master plan to cheat our way out of piano practice time.

> You cannot find what you are passionate about without being exposed to a variety of experiences.

Needless to say, our piano-playing skills did not improve much to the dismay of both our parents and our music teacher. Bewildered, they wondered why our skills never improved. After about three years of this charade we finally sat down with our parents and confessed to them that we didn't really like playing the piano. We did not, however, tell them that we'd been deceitful and pretended to practice.

Our parents were disappointed and tried to talk both of us into continuing the lessons. They did this by offering each of us $10 a month as an allowance, provided that we stuck with the piano and continued practicing. At nine years of age, what would you have done?

Well, you might have taken the higher ground, but we took them up on their offer! For another year, my brother and I continued to fake practicing the piano, and endured our weekly piano lessons and each received $120 for our sins. Despite being paid, it was an exhausting charade. It took each of us a further year of piano lessons to decide that, regardless of the money, we'd had enough. We had another conversation with our parents, spilled the beans and, fortunately for us, they let us off the hook.

In the meantime, I had begun focusing on mastering another skill— skiing. My experience on the ski team in Junior High had been about as different from playing the piano as anything could be. I loved skiing so much that I wished there had been more than the four scheduled practices each week.

One afternoon, looking very serious, my coach pulled me aside after a practice. "Listen, I know you've been breaking into the clubhouse and using the equipment," he said. I gulped, knowing I'd been busted!

You see, not only had I wanted more practice time, I had set about organizing it for myself. For several months, I had been breaking into the team clubhouse, after school, in order to borrow the gates. I'd take the gates up the ski lift and, by myself, set up my own courses. I would continue practicing until it was dark outside and then I would sneak the gates back into the clubhouse, thinking no one was any the wiser.

My coach continued, "You've got to stop doing that!" Just when I thought that I was about to be dropped from the team, he paused and smiled. "Here, he said," slipping a key into my hand. "Don't tell anyone that you have this, but start using it."

Ski racing was an activity I just couldn't keep myself out of. It was ridiculous really. Not only could I not get enough of it, if required, I was willing to commit minor felonies to feed my obsession with it. Skiing was pure play and I would have gladly spent every cent of my allowance to stay involved in the sport. How different this was from playing the piano where, in the end, I couldn't be paid to continue?

When I compare my experiences of skiing with those of playing the piano, I understand the nature of true passion. I also understand that spending time on activities about which we are not passionate is simply not sustainable, no matter how much we're getting paid.

> *Whenever I'm involved in an activity that I'm not passionate about, the best I can hope for is compliance, not commitment.*
>
> *What I do know is that when passion and talent intersect, magic happens!*

Whenever I'm involved in an activity that I'm not passionate about, the best I can hope for is compliance, not commitment. At the outset, I was able to comply with my parents' desire that I take piano lessons but, in the end, even that faded. Ski racing, on the other hand, was fuelled by a true commitment.

As a teenager and young adult, I was sufficiently lucky to be able to spend my career in ski racing. Since my competitive days, there have been other phases of my career when I haven't necessarily been quite as passionate about *what* I was doing, but I think I've always been able to be passionate about *why* I was doing what I was doing (such as supporting my family). In the short term, being passionate about the *why* can be enough. Over the long term, however, it is a guaranteed slow and painful death.

What I do know is that when passion and talent intersect, magic happens! It may sound crazy, but when we tune into what Joseph Campbell called our bliss, and explore possibilities, the universe opens up to support us. I have experienced this over and over again.

Think about your life. Let's turn to the dark side first to see if you can liberate some time and energy. Think about the times and situations where you tend to procrastinate. What do you need to be paid to do? Even better, what would you not do even if you were paid to do it? Are you currently involved in any of these energy-draining activities? Try to find ways to limit the time you spend on these activities. Would it be possible to delegate any of these activities or stop doing them altogether?

Now think about where you find joy. Where does passion exist for you? What would get you jumping out of bed each and every morning? What would you do with your time—for free? What is it that you just can't keep yourself out of? Look for ways that you can invite more of these activities into your life.

2.5

Are You Pushing Yourself To Death?

How To Regain Control And Get Your Life Back!

"I can't do this," I said. Tears welled up in my eyes. I looked in the mirror and my stomach sank. What I saw looking back frightened me. Skeleton-like, I was pale and gaunt. Trembling, I looked down into a sink full of hair that had fallen out of my head. "I just can't do this anymore."

I peered back up into the eyes of an unhappy man. A man with nothing left, no energy, no quality of life to speak of. I was killing myself with stress and indecision. Stress from the past six months, from the past year. I was working 80 hours a week; sun up to sun down every day. No vacation. In fact, no time off at all.

More than my health, my life was suffering. My wife and I rarely spoke—there was no time, and I knew she questioned this crazy life we were living. I couldn't blame her. Who wants to be married to a zombie?

How had I let things get this bad? I wondered. I knew the answer but I didn't want to face it. Facing it meant making some tough decisions, decisions that until now I hadn't been able to face. Staring into the mirror, I knew something had to change—and soon!

Truth be told, I wanted to run my own business. I wanted to share with others the lessons and strategies that I'd gained from a career in sport which I felt could help others, both in business and life in general. I've always felt that this was my calling, my passion. But rather than take the leap of faith needed to pursue my passion, I had chosen to work for a respected and exceedingly competitive corporation. A wonderful company, but one that was populated by ambitious, driven employees. People just like me.

> I've always displayed a tendency to push myself too hard and have needed people around me to say, "Hey, you've got to be patient, take it easy, pace yourself."

The last thing that I needed was an environment full of competitive, driven people like me! The truth was that my life lacked balance. Looking back to sport, the coaches with whom I did my best work were actually people who understood and endorsed the value of balance. They realized that some athletes needed to be pushed and some needed to be pulled back. I've always displayed a tendency to push myself too hard and have needed people around me to say, "Hey, you've got to be patient, take it easy, pace yourself."

A career decision had to be made. Was I going to leave the comfort and security of company employment and take the leap that—in my gut—I knew was right for me, or was I going to remain in my current position and die a slow, painful death?

So many emotions and fears weighed down on me. Guilt! My immediate supervisor had invested significant time, energy, and resources in me. The company had trained me, positioned me, and made my role an integral part of the company's marketing efforts. How was I going to tell my boss that I wanted to leave?

Fear also immobilized me, undermining my ability to take action and make a decision. I felt paralyzed both by my own fear of failure, as well as the fears and concerns expressed by my wife. Kristina was pregnant with our first child and I was currently the sole breadwinner in the household. How could I leave a secure position and predictable source of income and embark on the establishment of a new business without any guarantee of immediate cash flow? My wife, understandably, was very distressed. She was concerned about my health of course, but the fears evoked by her anticipation of an unpredictable future weighed heavily on her.

She knew that my current job wasn't a good fit for me and yet to see me embark upon a new venture, an entrepreneurial venture, was disquieting for her. She'd never been exposed to entrepreneurship. Her parents reinforced her fears. Her father had been a civil engineer with a steady paycheck, and her mother thought that I was crazy to consider leaving such a great job.

Fear and doubt were all around me. My own father questioned my sanity. "Gee," he said, "Do you really want to enter another field of employment as competitive as professional speaking and success coaching? Is that really what you want to do?"

Despite the doubts and fears of those around me, my gut instincts told me that I had to do this. I could no longer keep myself out of this field. Mustering up my courage, I asked for a meeting with the principal partners. Sitting in the boardroom, I shared my plans with them. Gracious people that they were, I was given a month to think about my future.

Grateful for their understanding and patience, I took the following month to consider my options. Over those four weeks, I experienced the return of my enthusiasm and energy and was able to confirm my decision to move on. I needed to lunge forward and start my business. I needed to pursue my purpose and my calling—sharing winning strategies to help other people succeed.

I lunged forward into entrepreneurship. The first few years were indeed tough. Despite my considerable assets at the outset, after two years I was $50,000 in debt in this venture. Regardless, I continued to trust my instincts and stuck with the process of building my own enterprise. I took risks that I needed to take, and I am happy to report that everything has worked out for the best and beyond anything that I could possibly have imagined. I presently book in excess of 50 speaking engagements annually and face the enviable task of choosing which offers to accept and which to decline.

It is a phenomenal feeling to be engaged in a venture about which I'm passionate and also for which I feel my greatest strengths and attributes are being fully utilized. In self-employment, I have the freedom I desire as well as the autonomy to decide what I will and will not do. In my entrepreneurial enterprise, I've found the perfect balance I long sought for. I feel blessed.

During my professional sports career, I espoused the following motto: success at all costs. I'd do anything—so long as it was both legal and ethical—in order to win, regardless of the personal costs. Success was often achieved to the detriment of my health, my friendships, and primary relationships. Now that I am married and a

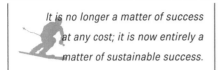

It is no longer a matter of success at any cost; it is now entirely a matter of sustainable success.

father, I am no longer willing to sacrifice such things. I am no longer willing to pursue success at any cost.

In my current business activities, I now practice a model which includes significant time off each year, and I've designed a more sustainable winning lifestyle. It is no longer a matter of success at any cost; it is now entirely a matter of sustainable success. Wouldn't you know it— with a more sustainable lifestyle model, I am more and more successful in all aspects of my life, including health and relationships!

Looking back, I realize that I should have paid attention to my gut instincts more promptly. I shouldn't have waited until everything I valued—my family, my marriage, and my health—were put at risk. I allowed others to push me while I continued to push myself. I allowed my own fears and the fears of others, however justified, to keep me from following my instincts and passions.

In not paying attention to my instincts, I invited far more negative stress into my life than would otherwise have been the case; so much so I literally pushed myself towards a premature death. Instead of following my passion and starting my own business, I was fiercely competing in a game which, to be honest, I wasn't really interested in playing. I had misplaced my loyalty and used it as an excuse to avoid making the final lunge forward. In misplacing my loyalty, I hurt not only my family, but also my employers because they didn't receive 100% effort and commitment from me.

I have witnessed how easy it is to get caught up in my own head, listening to fear and doubt instead of listening to my instincts and being accountable for my own happiness. I am reminded, time and time again, that each of us needs to follow our passion and extend ourselves on our own terms—but for the right reasons, our own reasons! All of us need to discover our own balance and develop our own model for success. This is crucial to living a winning life and having success in our pursuits, whatever they might be.

I wonder if you are avoiding making any critical decisions or living a life that runs counter to your gut instincts? Do you find yourself caving in to fear and doubt or are you going after a goal that truly motivates you? Are you leveraging your own strengths and passions or letting others determine what you should do with your life? Are you setting boundaries for yourself and others, determining what you are and are not willing to sacrifice in order to achieve success?

> *All of us need to discover our own balance and develop our own model for success. Listen to your gut instincts, establish your own boundaries, and lunge forward!*

I encourage you to embrace whatever challenges you see as an inevitable part of fulfilling your dreams and achieving your goals. Listen to your gut instincts, establish your own boundaries, and lunge forward!

Notes To Yourself

_____

_____

_____

_____

_____

_____

_____

_____

_____

_____

_____

_____

_____

_____

_____

_____

_____

_____

_____

_____

_____

_____

_____

_____

_____

_____

_____

_____

_____

_____

2.6

How Motivated By Materialism Are You?

Harnessing Your Materialism To Win

At 4:00 PM that afternoon, I had been awarded a World Cup trophy—something I had wanted for as long as I could recall. The trophy was beautiful. Two crystal spheres which sparkled like diamonds and worth more to me than any diamond. I stood on the podium beside my teammate, each of us claiming first and second position respectively. It was a phenomenal day for both of us. We had each accomplished something amazing. We'd achieved our best times ever and our entire team, our entire nation, had been rewarded with these two championship trophies. Years of sacrifice, hard work, and dedication had finally come to fruition.

By 5:00 PM, the press had swarmed around us, cameras clicking, flashbulbs popping, questions being tossed at us left and right. We were in our glory, so proud of ourselves and proud of the moment. The press asked us what we were going to do next. "Buy Harley Davidson motorcycles," we told them.

By 9:00 PM, we had moved the celebration back to our hotel. Family, friends, and teammates came to celebrate with us. My former coach and his wife traveled for three hours to join us in the celebration. It felt fantastic to have everyone who had a significant role in the outcome present and celebrating together, not only for our accomplishments in winning first and second place, but in acknowledging we had done so as a team.

By 9:30 PM, I decided to make my way upstairs to my hotel room to find a safe place for the trophy. I sat on the foot of my bed and held it in my hands, admiring the two crystal spheres and what they symbolized. I took a moment and congratulated myself for the years of commitment and hard work that had brought me to this moment.

> *What I had actually been chasing for all of those years was some tangible evidence of personal growth and improvement, not a trophy.*

Smiling, I set the trophy down on the tile floor and turned to go back to the party.

That's when the catastrophe happened. My pant leg caught on the trophy, and before I could react, the trophy hit the hard tile floor and shattered into pieces. I stood still, stunned in the middle of my hotel room staring at the shattered, emblematic remains of all the years of hard work and sacrifice. My whole life had been devoted to winning this trophy, and I had only been able to hold onto it for less than 6 hours. I couldn't believe it.

As I stood staring at the shattered remains of the trophy, a single thought occurred to me. "Well, the trophy is definitely destroyed and I can't change that. I can either cry about this or I can laugh." I had every reason in the world to cry, but instead I began to laugh. In fact, I laughed and laughed.

Shaking my head, I scooped the glass into a pile on the floor. Leaving it there, I left the room and I honestly didn't think about the trophy, shattered or otherwise, for the rest of the evening.

In that moment, when I burst into laughter, I finally realized the truth. For all those years, I believed I had been chasing the trophy, and the title. I had achieved that status and had the trophy in my hands—albeit fleetingly, I finally got it—all of my hard work wasn't about winning a trophy; it had been about pursuing a goal that would enable me to become the best I could be.

What I had actually been chasing for all of those years was some tangible evidence of personal growth and improvement, not a trophy. The journey to winning the World Cup was as important an accomplishment as the actual winning of the cup.

It sounds crazy, but even though the trophy had been destroyed, I knew at my core, that all my years of hard work and sacrifice could never be destroyed. The journey and the experiences were inside me. Who I was during those experiences and who I had become as a result had helped me to grow and develop in a

> *In focusing on your journey and staying in the moment, you will actually achieve your goal more quickly.*

way that no trophy ever could. That is what the goal does to the journey. In focusing on your journey and staying in the moment, you will actually achieve your goal more quickly.

The gifts that arise from embarking on the journey towards our stated goals... include self-awareness, learning to have confidence in ourselves, and giving our best effort. At its core, this is what winning is really about.

What I realize now is that while we need to be motivated in order to achieve our goals, whatever they may be (a trophy, money, a title), we are never fully defined by our accomplishments or the symbols of those accomplishments. We can experience and enjoy the external rewards of our efforts and accumulate material possessions which can define who we are or what we have accomplished but, like any external source of gratification, these measures of our accomplishments are both fragile and transient. Invest too much importance in them and our happiness will be temporary and our resilience becomes undermined.

Don't misunderstand me. Motivation, in the form of a clearly articulated goal, is a wonderful thing and often essential for achieving success; it's just not everything. It is what the setting of clear goals can do to enrich the journey that really matters. I now know that the process of achievement, not necessarily the symbols of achievement, is the true reward. The personal growth and the process that led to my accomplishments are what I really earned that day, and neither of these rewards could ever be broken or lost.

I wonder how frequently we get lost, confusing happiness with more tangible symbols of success. In the meantime, we are blind to the gifts that arise from embarking on the journey towards our stated goals. These gifts include self-awareness, learning to have confidence in ourselves, and giving our best effort. At its core, this is what winning is really about.

What about you? How are you living your life? Are you basing your happiness on material possessions as symbols of success? Are your identity and self-worth tied up in your last golf score, the size of your house, or the balance in your bank account? Have you made your happiness contingent upon your material situation (and therefore fragile) or are you focused on the process of personal growth and self-improvement?

Know that achievement and success are about growth. When you are being and doing your best, you can't help but reap the rewards.

3
Lunge Forward

A T ONE TIME OR ANOTHER, WE ALL EXPERIENCE FEAR. Fear can often defeat us. These are two indisputable facts. Many times I've discovered that despite picking a line, fear and doubt can still undermine our ability to achieve our goals. Learning how to overcome the paralysis caused by fear was one of the most valuable insights I learned during my sports career. I developed my own approach to overcoming fear and was able to learn how to stop fear from holding me back, so I could achieve the kind of results that more accurately reflected my capabilities. In many ways, the approach I developed for overcoming fears has been directly responsible for my success. More universally, my approach is also about personal change management—dealing with the uncertainty and ambiguity that change, especially sudden change, can provoke in any one of us. I have been told that it is one of the most powerful concepts I share with people. You are about to learn this powerful concept.

Lunging Forward is all about not letting our conscious and unconscious fears defeat us. It is about developing a proactive habit that enables us to move headlong into our fears and negative thoughts, overcoming our initial aversive response. Perhaps, most

> *Learning how to overcome the paralysis caused by fear was one of the most valuable insights I learned during my sports career.*

importantly, it is a way of being. When you recognize what is holding you back, you can learn to stop being victimized by fear and doubt and start winning instead. By embracing this secret, you'll learn to eliminate barriers, optimize your energy, stay a step ahead of the competition and feel tremendous personal satisfaction. You'll understand your reaction to fear, be able to better assess your options, and make decisions based on risk and reward.

> *When you recognize what is holding you back, you can learn to stop being victimized by fear and doubt and start winning instead.*

How well do you tend to handle anxiety and adversity? Do they affect your attitude? If plans or circumstances change just before the moment of execution, just before you push through the starting gate, can you embrace those changes and turn them into opportunities or do you let change overwhelm and perhaps unsettle you? Sometimes the mere thought of making a change, even a small change, can create undue anxiety and stress. As much as change can be unsettling, we need to change and adapt in order to be successful.

Often our fears can become ingrained, affecting both our behavior and what we choose to believe. If we remain blind to our beliefs and assumptions, if we close our minds to new possibilities, we lose out. The smallest unexplored beliefs or assumptions can prove to be our undoing. Conscious examination of all that we hold sacred can make all the difference. A belief or mindset as simple as, "In order to win, I need to be perfect," can definitely get in the way of our success.

Did you know that we can classify our fears into one of two types? There are primal fears related to survival, such as the fear of being bitten by a snake. There are also performance fears unrelated to survival, such as the fear of public speaking. Often we react to performance fears as if they were a matter of life or death. Physiologically, when we get up to speak in front of an audience, our body and mind can react as if we were in a life-threatening situation. We tremble, and choke, and turn a deep shade of red! If we were to pause, take a step back, and look at the actual risks associated with public speaking, we'd realize that we were quite safe, and unlikely to experience injury or death, even if we do perform poorly. How we react to performance fears may be a natural part of the fight or flight response, but it is far from optimal behavior.

> *If the potential rewards appear to be worth the risk, then jump in! Lunge Forward without fear and enjoy the process! After all, this is what life is really all about.*

I encourage you to take a step back before you execute your performance and assess the risks associated with the action you are about to take. Undertaking even an informal risk assessment will enable you to put your risks and possible rewards into a more realistic perspective. If the potential rewards appear to be worth the risk, then jump in! *Lunge Forward* without fear and enjoy the process! After all, this is what life is really all about.

85% of the world records set in sports were established by athletes who were performing with a conscious state of enjoyment?

Don't let those last minute, negative thoughts derail you from your goal. Learn to eliminate them! Empower yourself and give yourself the freedom and the permission to execute fully and with all the joy and passion that you deserve.

I learned, through many trials and errors, that life is a game. We are meant to enjoy it. Did you know that 85% of the world records set in sports were established by athletes who were performing with a conscious state of enjoyment? Enjoyment! That's what I'm talking about. Enjoyment! Passion! By eliminating fear and lunging forward, you will find more enjoyment and more passion in your life as you find yourself taking even greater risks. Enjoying the times that are challenging is a proven strategy to get more out of life.

The stories in this section share some deeply personal and powerful moments I've experienced over the years, both as an elite athlete and afterwards as a business owner and entrepreneur. There are moments of pain and moments of clarity, and collectively, they led me to realizing the secret of *Lunging Forward* which I'm eager to share with you now. As you read about these experiences, think about those areas of your life where you are *Lunging Forward*, as well as those areas where you are not but might begin to do so in order to fully embrace all that you are capable of being and becoming.

Lunge Forward into your winning life!

Notes To Yourself

_____

_____

_____

_____

_____

_____

_____

_____

_____

_____

_____

_____

_____

_____

_____

_____

_____

_____

_____

_____

_____

_____

_____

_____

_____

3.1

Lunge Forward Into Fear

What Happens When You Stop Taking Yourself So Seriously?

Kitzbühel, Austria is the site of the most feared and famed downhill venue in the world because of the steep, technical, and challenging nature of the course and terrain. In fact, more World Cup ski racers have crashed and been injured on this mountain than on any other, anywhere in the world.

Picture yourself as you slide out of the gate for your inspection run; you are amazed that it takes you 30 yards before you can stop. You stand there in disbelief, pounding your pole into the rock-solid ice. In Kitzbühel, members of the Austrian army are recruited to assist in preparing the course the night before a race; using fire hoses, they saturate the entire downhill course with water so that it freezes into sheer ice. As the military crew works the slope, moving over the freezing surface on their skis, they ensure that the surface is left rutted and uneven. When the racers come to ski the course, their skis will chatter and bounce around and the likelihood of a competitor loosing control has been made all the more likely, and all the more spectacular for the television viewers!

At Kitzbühel, you stand on a 45-degree slope. 6.2 seconds into the course you will be traveling at a speed of about 70 miles per hour when you hit the first jump that carries you about 70 yards through the air down the course. The major drawback on this top part of the course is that you can't actually see the landing zone from the point of take off. You must memorize the exact trajectory for your take off. Those of us who have skied at Kitzbühel have our own stories to tell about the need to take the right line. I was aware that the previous year, two racers had inadvertently taken the wrong line, sailed over the course fencing, and crashed into a barn!

As I stood in the start gate, my entire body was tight with the tension that came from knowing that I was about to travel at speeds in excess of 85 miles per hour on terrain that most people need ice axes to ascend. My mind was asking, "Can I do this? Have I done enough preparation and training? Have I taken any shortcuts?" Before I could answer these questions, my imagination began playing out the worst scenarios, anticipating all of the potential consequences.

I felt a heavy thud in my chest as the realization hit that I could end up paralyzed or maimed, just as some of my ski-racing peers had done on this very same mountain. I could even die. Plagued with doubts, I asked myself, "Is any of this worth it?" Another voice popped up presenting a different fear. "What if I can't muster the courage to move out of the start gate? What if I race and am so slow it's embarrassing?" I had trained to be here for 15 years, but I wondered if what I had done to get here would be enough.

I imagined disappointing my coaches and parents. I tried to convince myself that it was just another mountain, another course, but I knew that this was the most challenging course I had ever skied. Usually, on a World Cup course, my inner voice asked, "Which line will be the best?" Here at Kitzbühel, my mind asked, "Can I actually do this? Will I make it?" My throat was dry and I felt like I was going to vomit.

My long-term vision, "I want to win a World Cup," was clear in my mind though. I reminded myself that I had never known a World Cup Champion who hadn't raced at Kitzbühel. This race was a critical step in my development as a world-class competitive skier and I knew it. The catch was that I was also seriously wondering if I could make it to the bottom!

I pushed out of the start gate. Off the first jump I maneuvered the deadly Steilhang turn and missed the safety net by 2 inches. As I entered the final pitch, I bounced and chattered and crossed the finish line. To my elation, I had made it to the bottom and survived! Later on, at the hotel, together with the other rookie on the team, Luke Sauder, I put on the hit song "Alive," by Pearl Jam, and danced around to it elated to have made it down the course without injury or embarrassment.

As the initial thrill of actually finishing the race faded, I remembered that my goal was to do more than survive these races: it was to *win*!

That evening, I sat down for a video analysis session with my coach looking for ways to improve my performance. As I watched, I noticed that every time I hit a really fast, scary section in the course, I pulled back in fear, shifting my weight back onto my heels and slowed my speed down. I suddenly realized that my reaction to my fear was natural, but it was not optimal. I recognized that not only was I afraid, my reaction to my fear was limiting my performance.

> *I suddenly realized that my reaction to my fear was natural, but it was not optimal. I recognized that not only was I afraid, my reaction to my fear was limiting my performance.*

I became aware that I needed to retrain my reaction to my fear since my current reaction was not serving me well. Going forward, when I next ventured out onto the mountain and hit a really fast, scary section, I trained myself to Lunge Forward. I practiced this day after day in each training session. After a while, I started to seek out everyday opportunities to practice this new reaction to fear. I was constantly retraining and conditioning this lunge forward response.

After 5 years of retraining and reconditioning, I headed back to Kitzbühel. It was a difficult year. The conditions were challenging and 8 of the first 15 racers had been flown to the local hospital by helicopter. Nevertheless, I stood in the start gate confident because of all the training and conditioning I had undertaken to *Lunge Forward* into my fears. I stepped through the start gate and blasted onto the course. As I crossed the finish line less than two minutes later, I looked up and realized that I had just set a new World Cup downhill course record in Kitzbühel of 97 miles per hour (151.5 kilometres per hour). I realized that the prize was on the other side of my fear. We need to lunge in and grab that prize. We need to train ourselves to *Lunge Forward.*

As I reflect on my Kitzbühel experiences, which took place over a period of five years, I realize that there were two distinct aspects to my fear. One aspect was the fear that I might not survive. While this fear was real, it was not nearly as debilitating as the other aspect … the fear that put doubt in my mind about the quality

> *I realized that the prize was on the other side of my fear. We need to train ourselves to Lunge Forward.*

of my performance. This is the fear behind the voice that whispered in my ear, "After spending all of your life to get here, you will not be able to do this. You will be too afraid to race. Even if you do, you will be too slow." This is the voice that warned me I didn't have what it took to live up to my own expectations, never mind the expectations of my coaches and parents. This is the voice that brought the burden of guilt in knowing what these people had sacrificed for me so that I might have the chance, the opportunity, to race, and overwhelmed me with the fear that my performance would now let them down.

I so desperately wanted to prove myself to all of the people who had supported me. I had always thought of myself as being extremely courageous. In the days leading up to my first race at Kitzbühel, back in 1992, I had wondered how my image might be tainted if I was not able to bring myself to ski the course. I felt both my identity and my reputation as a professional athlete were at stake.

> We all have fears that are limiting our thoughts and our actions. If we don't identify and admit to these fears, then we are at the mercy of our natural reactions.

If I didn't race, everyone would think I was a coward. If I did race but performed poorly, my coaches might question their decision to have me race the course. It was hard to admit that I was still seeking approval from others, but it was true. Instead of facing the challenge ahead of me, I was caught in an all or nothing mindset. I thought, "Either I race this course like a champion or I hold back and I lose." As a man in my twenties, I had never admitted to myself that I had fears. At Kitzbühel, I was faced with several fears that were too obvious to dismiss. I finally had to admit my fears to myself so that I could move beyond them. Over time, I learned to identify my performance fears and understand where they were coming from—all necessary personal work before I could face those same fears head on.

Now you probably don't plan on racing Kitzbühel anytime soon, but how can you benefit from this same approach? We all have fears that are limiting our thoughts and our actions. If we don't identify and admit to these fears, then we are at the mercy of our natural reactions. We want to take charge of our reactions. Unidentified fears are invisible handcuffs shackling our potential.

Think about a fear that is holding you back from achieving your full potential. I assure you, at this very moment, you have a fear that is limiting you in some

> *We want to take charge of our reactions. Unidentified fears are invisible handcuffs shackling our potential.*

way. Is the fear holding you back a fear of failure? Is it a fear of rejection? Is it a fear of appearing foolish, uninformed, or unknowledgeable? Perhaps it is a fear of not being liked? How about a fear of success? These fears, and so many others, are what holds us back from winning. So, what do we do? You need to follow the four step approach for *Lunging Forward* that I applied in Kitzbühel. These four steps are:

1. Identify your Fear
2. Identify your Risk-to-Reward Ratio
3. Lunge Forward
4. Enjoy the Challenge

The focus here is on the first step, to identify your fear. Kitzbühel taught me that there are two kinds of fear: those that relate to our survival and those that relate to our performance. Fears related to our survival usually arise over risks where our physical safety and sense of security are in jeopardy. My fears about sustaining injury or dying on the mountain at Kitzbühel are examples of survival fear that are as real as a fear of being attacked when walking alone late at night in an unsafe neighborhood. If we are faced with a survival fear, then we need to take it very seriously. We need to know the facts and not move forward out of blind optimism. The greater the risk, the more reality-based thinking we require. We need to take survival fears more seriously.

Performance fears, on the other hand, are rarely life threatening and are often experienced in social situations. Universal examples include a fear of failure, of rejection, of not reaching our potential, of not being

> *There are two kinds of fear: those that relate to our survival and those that relate to our performance.*
>
> *It is performance fears that we need to lunge forward into.*

perfect. It was a surprising revelation to me to discover that my performance fears loomed larger than my survival fears at Kitzbühel. Performance fears evoke just as much stress as do survival fears, and too much stress has a negative impact on our performance and our results. However, the negative outcomes we wish to avoid when we become preoccupied or fearful about our performance are not usually life threatening and are rarely as severe as those associated with survival fears. It is performance fears that we need to *lunge forward* into. These are the fears that we face daily. We need to identify these fears and be able to take them *less* seriously.

What happens if we don't identify our performance fears and instead let them hold us back? Instead of being guided by our intention and potential, we remain at the mercy of our natural reaction to avoid fear. We inadvertently end up avoiding the challenge inherent in striving to reach our goals. In not identifying the fears we carry with us, we burden ourselves with stress and undermine our ability to do what we need to do in order to succeed. We also prevent ourselves from performing to the best of our abilities. Performance fears eat away at us, undermining our health, our potential, and even our pocket book. They rob us of our confidence and make our responses and reactions far from optimal. We do not need to be at the mercy of our unidentified fears and automatic reactions to those fears. Identifying our fears helps us to be purposeful about what we do want to bring into our life—*winning*! However you define winning, recognizing your fears will help you succeed.

Take a few minutes and think about some of the fears that you are carrying around. Name a fear that you have right now that is impeding your progress. Name another fear that is holding you back from doing what you need to do. How is this fear showing up in your life? What do you think is at the core of this fear? What would change in your life if you no longer had this fear?

For the next two weeks, pay attention to any feelings of fear that you experience. Be on the lookout for

> *Identifying our fears helps us to be purposeful about what we do want to bring into our life—winning! However you define winning, recognizing your fears will help you succeed.*

situations or activities that cause you to become apprehensive. Tune in to your senses to identify when and where you experience anxiety, stress, and fear in your life. This exercise will help you recognize those fears that limit your performance ability. This is the first step towards changing your future thinking and actions. In the next story, we'll explore what you can do once you have identified your fears.

Notes To Yourself

3.2

A Proven Strategy To Get More Out Of Life

How To Invite More Energy, Love And Success Into Your Life

I woke from a deep sleep at 6:00 AM to find Kristina, my wife, leaning against our dresser. Clutching her stomach, she was panting rapidly. Wiping the sleep from my eyes, I grabbed our stopwatch and began doing what I had learned to do—time the contractions. They were long and strong. Less than four minutes apart. My heart hammered in my chest. It was time. My wife was in labor.

I quickly phoned our family doctor to tell him we were on our way to the hospital, and then, grabbing our bags, we headed out the door. Doctors and nurses swarmed around us as soon as we arrived at the hospital. "Yes, it's time," they said, as they conducted tests and monitored her vital signs. I was so excited; our baby was on the way!

Thirty-five interminable hours later, those very same doctors and nurses had done everything to my poor Kristina. They'd poked and prodded her beyond human tolerance. She'd had Pitocin, she'd had an epidural, they'd broken her water, they'd put water back in. Nothing! No baby! Just pain!

Standing helpless, I watched my wife endure another contraction. As the contraction subsided, a little smile appeared on her face. "What?" I asked, confused.

"I feel like a satellite dish," she said, holding up her arms. "Look at me. I have wires coming out of my arms, wires coming out of my legs. I'm a satellite dish only I don't know what kind of reception I'm trying to bring in," she said with a laugh. I cannot imagine how she managed to laugh but I was most grateful for it.

A few minutes later our doctor walked in. His face stern and serious, he recommended that Kristina have a C-section. Kristina began to cry.

I tried to console her as I recounted all of the positive aspects of having a C-section we'd learned in prenatal classes. I reminded her that it was the best way to keep both her and the baby safe and healthy. While I was doing my best to console my wife, internally, I was in a state of near panic. All I could think about were all of the things that could go wrong.

My wife was in so much pain, both physically and emotionally. All I wanted to do was to be able to take her pain away. I wanted to be able to reduce the obvious distress she was feeling. As I stood there, trying to console her, I'm sure that she was picking up on all of my doubts and fears.

The doctor came back into the room for our answer. "Doctor," my wife said wiping her eyes dry. "Can I ask you a question?" He nodded. "If your wife were in the same situation as me, would you recommend this for her?"

Stunned, the doctor took a step back. "Wow," he said. "No one has ever asked me that." He paused for a moment. "Yes," he said. "Yes, I would recommend that she do that."

My wife got that little smile on her face again. "Hold on," she said. "I'd better qualify that question. How are you and your wife getting along in your relationship?"

The laughter that filled the room was an instant release of tension. The stress evaporated thanks to Kristina and her capacity for joy. Thanks to her capacity to go with the flow and enjoy life, regardless of what it throws at you. Here Kristina was faced with the biggest challenge of her life and somehow she found a way to enjoy the challenge. In doing so, she made it a lot easier, and ultimately more enjoyable for the rest of us. She flowed with the moment, with the challenge, and we all functioned better as a result.

Twenty minutes later our little baby boy, our little miracle, was born. We named him Colby. "Cary," the doctor said, handing me my son. "Enjoy your son. And with that wife of yours..." His smile grew to a grin and he shook his head, "Have a long and happy life."

Throughout the ordeal of the birth of our baby, Kristina managed to exemplify one of the many characteristics of great leadership. She set an example for the rest of us by finding a way to enjoy the challenge, a challenge which also happened to be more difficult for herself than it was for anyone else.

When I look at my own performance during Kristina's labor, I could have done so much better. I was so stressed, and afraid, and worried about my wife and my baby that I wanted to throw up. I certainly wasn't enjoying the process. It was such a strange predicament for me to be in—watching someone I loved having to bear so much pain and uncertainty and my feeling so utterly powerless to intervene. I wanted so much to take the pain and stress away from my wife and take it on myself, but that wasn't possible and it wasn't what she really needed. She needed fun, entertainment, and energy.

Instead of thinking, "What can go wrong?," it would have been so much better if I had focused on, "What does she need from me in this moment?" I needed to stop taking the situation and myself so seriously. If only I could have relaxed and had a little fun, it would have helped Kristina to enjoy the experience more fully.

> *We perform more successfully when we're relaxed and our mind is calm. Our demeanor can also have a positive effect on those around us; other people will also give a better performance as a result of the example we set.*

That day, I learned that it's not always the best thing to be too serious when it's time to perform. There is value in trying to find the humor in what, at least initially, feels like a difficult situation. Despite the life-changing circumstances—the birth of our son—I don't always remember to apply the lesson I learned that day, but I am trying.

We perform more successfully when we're relaxed and our mind is calm. Our demeanor can also have a positive effect on those around us; other people will also give a better performance as a result of the example we set. You may have heard that like attracts like. When we perform with confidence, and radiate or project our energy in a relaxed way, we actually attract those people who have the same or a similar capacity, and they can make excellent colleagues, associates, clients, and team members. In turn, we are all able to perform more successfully and achieve better results.

Think about your own life. Are you able to enjoy the challenges that life gives you? Are you having fun, even just a little bit, during the tough situations? Are you able to let go of stress and enjoy life?

Notes To Yourself

3.3

Stop Avoiding Success!

When Being Too Slow To Change
Stands In The Way Of Your Success

With my ski boots on my feet, I stepped into my bindings and looked down the snow-covered slope of the mountain. I was preparing to test a technological development, and to be honest, I was more than a little skeptical.

Taking a deep breath, I pushed forward, not at all confident that the experiment was worthy of my time or involvement. However, a wonderful thing happened on my way down the mountain. I took the first step in learning a valuable lesson, a lesson that I now carry with me every day.

A fellow ski racer, Marc Girardelli, had inspired the source of this lesson. Marc had been doing well on the World Cup Giant Slalom circuit, winning events all season. People were noticing his victories, myself included. What some of us had also noticed was the new device he was using on his skis—something called the Derby Flex.

The Derby Flex is a rubber plate covered with aluminum, originally designed to combat joint pain and fatigue in recreational skiers. It is fastened between the ski and the binding and supposedly offered a smoother ride down the hill.

The paradox was that conventional wisdom dictated that in order to get the fastest ride, you needed to be close to the snow. People have even shaved down their skis and their boot soles in order to get closer to the snow. Attaching something that lifted you up and further way from your ski was in direct conflict with the accepted wisdom.

For years, I had operated under the same assumption, never questioning it. Now, I had agreed to get involved with the testing of a new concept because the sport demanded it. Once people realized how

Marc was winning, everyone and their brother began attaching the Derby Flex plate to their skis. To remain competitive, I had to follow suit.

As things turned out, the risers did work and proved to improve performance. I was able to carve a better turn and make it down a course in a significantly faster time. I adopted the technology, installing it first on my giant slalom skis but not, for some reason, on any of my downhill skis. Of course, not everyone was as slow to adopt the technology as I had been. Before long, some racers were using the technology on downhill gear. Again, I had to follow, just to keep up with the competition.

Slow to accept change, I finally tried the risers on my downhill skis and had my best race of the season. I began to see the light. I recognized that my reluctance in embracing and adapting to new technology had cost me dearly, in terms of better results at early season events.

Thankfully, I began to learn from my earlier hesitation. At the North American Championships I noticed that one racer had two risers on his skies in the giant slalom. Instead of dismissing it, or waiting for everybody else to try it first, I decided to try it right away. I ended up winning my first North American Championship in the giant slalom, generally not my best event.

I then went on to become the first person to try double risers in the World Cup Downhill events. I experienced fantastic results and achieved three World Cup podium finishes that year. More people caught on to the two-riser approach, only this time I had been a leader instead of a follower.

If we're always slow to adopt and adapt to change, including the change brought by...new technologies, we run the risk not of merely struggling to keep up but perhaps of being completely left behind.

This experience highlighted how important it is to consider adopting new technologies and new ways of thinking quickly—instead of holding on, steadfastly, to old beliefs and paradigms. Almost faster than we can keep up with them, new technologies, theories, and techniques are developed that hold potential for us to better our performance, become more efficient and, potentially, achieve greater success. If we're always slow to adopt and adapt to change, including the change brought by the introduction of new technologies, we run the risk not of merely struggling to keep up but perhaps of being completely left behind.

Take a look at your life. I invite you to look at your beliefs, concepts, and practices, as well as the technologies you use, and see if there is anything you are stubbornly holding on to which might be holding you back. Are you clinging to the familiar because it is easier than embracing change? In what areas of your life has your own stubborn sense of doing things as you have always done them, of insisting that your way is the right way, become more important than being successful?

I challenge you to be more open-minded to new thinking. It is a critical step for anyone of us striving to achieve our next success or breakthrough. Study new innovations and technologies and be quick to test and adopt them.

Notes To Yourself

_____

_____

_____

_____

_____

_____

_____

_____

_____

_____

_____

_____

_____

_____

_____

_____

_____

_____

_____

_____

_____

_____

_____

_____

_____

_____

_____

_____

3.4

Are You Shackled By Perfection?

How Escaping Perfection Will Help You Win

Gary Brook, a friend of mine, recently asked me a strange question. "Cary, you spent most of your life training hard with an intense focus on international ski racing. I apologize if this question seems a trifle blunt, but why didn't you win a World Cup earlier in your career?"

While it seems crazy to me to think that I might have achieved my goal sooner, I knew immediately that this was true. I thought about Gary's question for a minute and replied, "Before I was able to win, I had to first understand what was holding me back from becoming a champion." There were two issues and they were linked.

"The first issue was that I needed to learn to allow myself to experience flow so that I could perform to the best of my abilities when it mattered most—on race day. I actually needed to stop trying so hard and stop forcing my performance on the day of a competitive event. I had to stop getting in my own way and instead enjoy the challenge. The second and most important issue that kept me from winning was not being aware of the beliefs that were actually holding me back."

Gary's brow furrowed as he interrupted me, asking, "Wait a second, how can a belief hold you back?" "Let me try and explain," I said. "I was surprised to discover that I had a limiting belief requiring that everything be *perfect* in order for me to win. Believe me, this apparently insignificant, subconscious belief was a literal brick wall keeping me from race victories. I had idealized winning to the extent that if anything, no matter how small, went awry in my warm-up runs, I thought, 'I cannot possibly win now.' I believed

> *I needed to learn to allow myself to experience flow so that I could perform to the best of my abilities when it mattered most.*

87

> *The...most important issue that kept me from winning was not being aware of the beliefs that were actually holding me back.*

that if I wasn't skiing perfectly on every single training run the morning of a race, then there was no way that I could win." Gary was nodding his head now, beginning to understand how I had shackled myself by perfection.

I continued to explain this belief to Gary. "First of all, the idea of 'perfection' is as impossible in ski racing as it is in most other areas in life. There are so many changing variables that require spur of the moment adjustments that it makes it truly impossible to deliver a flawless performance. I'm reminded here to share that our beliefs don't always need to make sense to us and yet we still hold onto them! Holding onto my belief that *I needed to be perfect to win* was not serving me well. I was carting around this impossible goal of being perfect—and it was stressing the heck out of me!"

Gary was smiling and said, "Trying to be perfect has never really worked for me either." I replied, "Do you know the upside in my striving for perfection during training? It was actually good for me because I developed my ability to focus, more so than many of my competitors, and became adept at mastering all of the variables that you need to be aware of in order to win a race. On race day though, trying to be perfect was hurting my performance because I was so afraid of making a mistake. Practice makes perfect, but competing is not about perfection—it is about executing your best performance in the moment. Once I became aware of my belief, I was able to look at both training and race situations more objectively. I looked ahead and realized that if I continued to require that everything be 'perfect,' I was never going to win."

> *Practice makes perfect, but competing is not about perfection it is about executing your best performance in the moment.*

"I began the process of changing this belief. I realized that on race day it didn't matter if something went wrong in the warm-up or the training runs—there were really only two minutes that mattered! (Most downhill ski races take less than two minutes to complete.) Once I was able to look at the limitations of my belief and find a new perspective, I was able to begin retraining myself to race more freely on race day. It was truly liberating to finally free myself of this self-imposed burden which I had been carrying around for a long time."

Perfection is an impossible standard. It can be a helpful ideal to strive for in practice, but it is always an unrealistic standard in performance.

"The stress I had experienced dissipated like a barbell being taken off my shoulders and I felt free and light. I was no longer restricted by my fear of making a mistake. Instead, knowing that with all of my preparation, my best would be enough energized me; I didn't need to try to be more than who I was in the moment. I had to lunge forward into my fear of not doing things perfectly. By adopting some new winning beliefs, such as, 'I strive for success rather than perfection,' I was able to advance through the national rankings and win numerous national and international titles including a World Cup in Aspen, Colorado."

Gary asked me, "How about the World Cup race, did you ski perfectly then?" "No, I made a few mistakes. That's what's so interesting. Perfection is an impossible standard. It can be a helpful ideal to strive for in practice, but it is always an unrealistic standard in performance."

I went on to tell Gary how my becoming aware of the beliefs that kept me from winning in competitive sport had been just the beginning. I explained, "Since then, I have discovered other beliefs which have held me back from success in other areas of my life. Regarding my financial goals, for instance. I always wanted to make more money. After examining my beliefs about money I realized that, deep down, I believed 'The more money I make, the busier I will be and I will have to manage greater responsibilities.'"

"Once I was aware of this belief, I embarked upon consciously changing the way in which I thought about money and the acquisition of wealth. I imagined how hard my life would become without any money. I began to see how my life was actually made easier by having more money. I started examining my own life, looking for

Changing my core belief from 'more money makes life more difficult' to 'the more money I make, the easier my life gets,' also made a significant difference to my ability to attract and accept money.

proof of the opposite truth, that having more money would mean a more carefree life and, ultimately, an easier life. For instance, I could change the oil in my car, clean my house or mow the lawn myself, or I could pay someone to do these things for me and instead spend that time with my children. Money allows me to take vacations; it allows me to hire people to do many things that I don't necessarily enjoy. I formed a new winning belief that I read each morning as part of my daily routine: 'The more money I make, the easier my life gets.'"

"As a result of my changed attitude about money, my income doubled within the year. I am sure there were many other variables that had an impact on my success that same year. However, changing my core belief from 'more money makes life more difficult' to 'the more money I make, the easier my life gets,' also made a significant difference to my ability to attract and accept money." Gary looked deep in thought and said, "I wonder what beliefs I'm carrying around that are holding me back."

As I write this, I can't help but wonder which of your beliefs are keeping you from being more successful in your life. Identifying your limiting beliefs is a technique you can use to improve all areas of your life—finances, relationships, sales, leadership, parenting, health, fitness, sleep—virtually anything. Unless you are already achieving everything you want in life, I urge you to take a moment and look inside and ask yourself the following two questions. What beliefs are holding me back from achieving more of what I desire? What alternative beliefs could I adopt that would help me to be more successful?

3.5

Boost Your Productivity 100% Overnight

What Would You Do With An Extra 28 Hours In Your Week?

It was a perfect day to be on the beach in Puerto Vallarta. The sun was warming the clear blue ocean and sparkles of white light danced on the crests of the waves. I was on vacation and all my family was with me. So why was I so unbelievably annoyed?

I had been reading Donald Trump's book, *Think Like a Billionaire*. In it, he states the reason for his success was due to his habit of only sleeping four hours each night. This seemed to me to be one of the most unreasonable competitive advantages I'd ever heard of. As a professional athlete, I had done some crazy things in order to be the best, but this lack of sleep seemed downright ridiculous. In fact, the whole idea of it just annoyed me.

The following week, that same feeling of aggravation hit me again. I was reading *Fantastic*, a biography of Arnold Schwarzenegger. In a section describing his typical daily routine, Schwarzenegger speaks of his habit of waking at 5:00 AM after sleeping just five hours. I was thinking, "Here's yet another successful guy who appears to be completely unreasonable about his pattern of sleep. Was this merely coincidence?"

The fact that both Donald Trump and Arnold Schwarzenegger were highly successful and effective made some sense; they were able to get more done in the time most of us spend sleeping. It made sense to me, and yet I was thoroughly annoyed about having learned this information.

Why was I so annoyed? It was because I need lots of sleep. For as long as I can remember I have needed eight or nine hours of sleep. As a child, typically I'd put my pajamas on and crawl into my bed without being told it was time to do so. As a full-time athlete, I also needed a lot of sleep. In fact, if I didn't get sufficient rest, I had a tendency to get headaches.

Suddenly, a funny thought hit me, "As a child and an athlete, I had a growing and recovering body. Might it be different for me now that I was an adult? "Over time, could I train myself to get by with less sleep and, if so, how well would I function?" My aggravation turned to excitement. "What if it were possible for me to spend an extra 4 hours a day in gainful activity instead of sleeping?" I wondered.

I decided I had nothing to lose by trying to learn to get by on less sleep. I searched the internet and found an e-book called *Powerful Sleep* by Kacper Postawski on how to sleep less and have more energy. I purchased a copy immediately and printed it out.

Determined to master Postawski's techniques, I got up the next morning at 4:00 AM and started to read his book. I felt exhausted, but soon reached a paragraph that really got my blood pumping. Postawski claims that most of us sleep too much for no good reason. He argues that the greatest single factor influencing our tendency to oversleep is our erroneous belief that we actually need that much sleep.

Here was yet another person who appeared to be unreasonable, but I was getting used to it by now. In fact, I was ready to become more unreasonable myself.

Postawski's research was fascinating and, although not all of the tips in his book worked for me, some of them have been fantastic.

I have been sleeping four to five hours for at least four nights each week for the past six months now. It was difficult in the beginning (and I found I needed to take a couple of naps during the day), but I have now conditioned myself to be effective with this new routine.

As you might imagine, my productivity has shot through the roof (100s of percentage points) and my life is more balanced. I am able to accomplish so much more in the four extra hours of uninterrupted time between 4:00 and 8:00 AM. In addition, I am able to spend a greater proportion of time with my family. The true bonus is that I have learned more about my capacity to be unreasonable.

The reason I read Trump's book in the first place was to uncover a new strategy for winning. There was also a part of me that suspected that perhaps he possessed some kind of unfair genetic advantage and my knowing that would enable me to let myself off the hook for not being a billionaire just like him.

The last thing I had wanted to learn was that Donald Trump attributed his success to following a daily routine that seemed completely unreasonable and counter to my beliefs.

> The fact is that life is unreasonable. The more unreasonable we are with life, the more it tends to give us the results we want. Too often, we hold on to "reasonable beliefs" and expect extraordinary results.

The fact is that life is unreasonable. The more unreasonable we are with life, the more it tends to give us the results we want. Too often, we hold on to "reasonable beliefs" and expect extraordinary results.

For me, my reasonable belief was that I needed eight to nine hours of sleep each night. While I had got as far as questioning whether my belief was valid, I had never fully challenged it for a consistent period of time or determined whether in hanging on to the notion that I needed as much sleep as eight to nine hours every night could be limiting my effectiveness.

These types of beliefs are what I call "unquestioned beliefs." We have inherited them from our parents, our friends, as a result of our socialization and cultural environment. Such beliefs as these, if they go unchallenged, remain in our subconscious, where they can interfere with our ability to become all that we are capable of becoming.

When it came to my sleep habits, I had simply been on autopilot. My belief about the amount of sleep that I needed was a limiting belief. Once I questioned my unconscious belief about sleeping, my life changed.

I wonder if you have any unquestioned beliefs that do not improve your ability to win but are still guiding your life? Like me, it may be time to renew yourself by shaking up your routines and opening up to new experiences.

What small changes can you make to your daily routine to invigorate yourself? How could you extend the "unreasonable" mindsets held by Trump or Schwarzenegger to become more extraordinary in your life? Don't misunderstand me, I'm not suggesting that you necessarily sleep less. That would be unreasonable! Besides, what would *you* do with all of that extra time?

Notes To Yourself

3.6

The Secret To Living A Winning Life

*What It Takes To Stop Breaking Promises To Yourself
And Start Making The Most Of Your Life*

I was in a VIP lounge at O'Hare Airport, in Chicago, gripping the phone as my hands shook. Suddenly, the entire room was blurry. Tears were streaming down my face. My cousin, Chad, was on the other end of the phone sharing the most horrible news.

The previous night, my teammate and long-time friend, Rob Bosinger, had died in his sleep from a cardiac arrest. His death came completely out of the blue; he was just 39 years old and had no history of heart problems. He left behind a wife and a 6-month-old son, Matts. My mind was racing as the tears streamed down my face. I thought about what an amazing man Rob had been. He was so fun-loving and friendly towards everyone. It had always been a sheer joy to be around Rob. I thought about his wife, Janet, and how she had lost the love of her life. I tried to imagine what becoming a widow at such a young age would be like for her and my heart sank. Then my thoughts turned to their son, Matts, who had been robbed of the opportunity to grow up knowing his own father. It all seemed so unfair.

Rob's death felt very close to home for me. Rob's wife, Janet, and my wife, Kristina, had been pregnant at the same time. Our daughter, Linnea, was born just two weeks before Matts. It didn't take long for me to start imagining what would happen if I had been the one who had died that evening. I thought about not being able to watch my children grow up and become happy and successful adults. I felt devastated when I contemplated not being around to witness my children learning to walk, or their first day of school, or their first date.

I wondered how Matts would cope with never being able to learn life lessons from his father, as I had learned from my own father. As a child, I had been able to witness my father's strong work ethic and deep respect for other people, both of which have had a profound influence on who I am today. I was fortunate to grow up in a family with two parents and gain knowledge through observing their very different ways of being. I realized that Matts would never know Rob's gentle nature or learn, first hand, anything about his philosophy of life. Matts would never be able to observe his father in action and use this knowledge to help him discover himself and what he might be capable of becoming. Worse still, this little boy would never receive the gift of confidence that comes from the direct experience of having his father love and support him unconditionally. I pictured Matts, at age 6, with absolutely no recollection of how much love his father had for him and I felt weak and inconsolable.

I was comforted, somewhat, by my unshakeable belief that someday Matts would be able to make meaning of his father's death, as well as any of us are able to find gifts in the darkest of life events, over which none of us has absolute control. I also knew Janet would ensure as best she could, that Rob's legacy would be shared with Matts as he grew up.

I continued to reflect upon Rob's death and my own mortality over the next few days. I asked myself, "What would I regret if I died right now? What haven't I done? How might these regrets and deficits be impacting my children?" It hit me that I had been deferring living and deferring having fun until later. I wondered to myself, "What if later never comes?" In a moment of reflection, I realized that I deferred gratification far more than most people I knew. While I believed that my ability to defer immediate gratification had been a key factor in my past success, I also realized I had become 'too good' at deferring gratification. I needed to enjoy the now, right now, and stop postponing all the fun until later. The question for me wasn't, 'When am I going to die?' but rather, 'When am I going to start living?'

> *The question for me wasn't, 'When am I going to die?' but rather, 'When am I going to start living?'*

I remembered the promise I had made to myself several years before. I had been so nervous before a World Cup ski race I had made myself a promise in order to relax: I would buy myself a Harley Davidson motorcycle if I made it onto the World Cup podium. On that occasion, I did make it onto the podium, but I postponed buying the Harley until much later.

By the time summer rolled around, I was preoccupied nursing damaged knees and it wasn't a good time to buy a motorbike. Another ski season came and went and another summer rolled around. I was feeling frustrated because my results had slipped due to my sore knees, so again, I didn't buy the bike. Instead, I bought a house and then it didn't seem very practical to buy my Harley. After that, well I can't even remember the excuse. Every time I thought about actually buying my motorbike I decided that the time was not right, right now, and it would be better to wait until another time. The right time to follow through on this promise to myself was always at some undetermined, future point when everything in my life would indicate that it was the perfect time!

As silly and insignificant as it may sound, the more I thought about Rob dying prematurely, the more that Harley Davidson seemed to be tugging at my gut. This is a perfect example of something fun, which I had been deferring. Recognizing that I had not only broken promises to myself, but that I had also become an expert at denying myself fun, I couldn't help thinking, "What kind of role model was I really being for my children? What messages—conscious or otherwise, were they learning from me about how to live their lives? How would this example of an unlived part of my life, if I failed to change my outlook in this regard, eventually impact who they would become?"

Rob's death made me realize that I had spent most of my life being afraid of investing my time, energy, or money into things that don't necessarily help me achieve my long-term goals. My need to achieve is so strong that I have told myself that it is not only OK but it is necessary to defer enjoying my life until some future time.

Let me give you a few further examples. I have always been reluctant to go out occasionally to a comedy club or to have more frequent dinner parties because I need to save my energy and my focus for work. I have been too afraid of wasting valuable, *productive* time over something frivolous like riding a motorbike. I have been scared of spending my money on anything that might not fund my long-term dreams and actually help me acquire *more money*. I realized that I had forgotten that life is about more than counting money and achieving goals. It seemed that no matter what finish line I crossed, no matter what I accomplished, no matter what material possession I acquired; I still wanted something more. I had taken my goal achievement so seriously that I ended up taking my life too seriously.

When I thought about Rob, I thought about how much fun he had and how he had loved motorbikes. I said to myself, "That's it. I'm buying my bike. Rob would approve." Within two weeks of Rob's passing, I called my cousin to come over and see my brand new 2003 custom Harley Davidson chopper. I believe that Rob's message to me was, "Cary, enjoy the now. Quit delaying living."

I have finally surrendered to the fact that I am going to die someday and it might be sooner than I would like, so I better enjoy what I have right now. Since that day in the Chicago airport, I have been deliberate about making sure my life is about more than being productive and achieving my goals. I want my children to experience their father as being someone who values fun in the same way he values achievement.

My Harley is an example of just one step towards a more conscious commitment to enjoy my life more fully. My motorbike is silly, foolish, frivolous, impractical and purely for fun. And that is exactly why I bought it—to be sillier, more foolish, more frivolous and less practical. I need to have some fun *now*! Whenever I ride my bike, it serves as a reminder for me to relax and enjoy life, and I think of Rob and of living my life in the present moment. The purchase of my Harley was my first tangible step toward *Lunging Forward* to enjoyment.

What has been surprising for me is that even though I have recently dedicated more time to having fun, I am achieving more and producing better results in every area of my life. I also have more energy. Taking time for fun has recharged me and kept me invigorated.

I realize now that if we want to truly live a winning life, then we need to enjoy what we do. We don't serve anyone very well by deferring happiness. Worse still, we might die before we finally cash in the 'enjoyment chips' that we have been saving. When we have fun, we get more out of life. The people around us are inspired by our enthusiasm for life. When we are truly engaged in life, we are also more likely to attract the right people and resources to help us succeed.

I wonder if any of this rings true for you. Is there a promise that you've made to yourself that you haven't yet followed through upon? Are you deferring having fun? Are you being too practical? Are you deferring living until later? What impact do you want to have upon your children and your loved ones? What will it take before you finally start living?

> *If we want to truly live a winning life, then we need to enjoy what we do. We don't serve anyone very well by deferring happiness...we might die before we finally cash in the 'enjoyment chips' that we have been saving.*

If we don't start living, we lose our zest for life and we might just miss out on the best thing of all: our own life! Honor the promises that you have made to yourself.

Notes To Yourself

4

Be Resilient

To WIN IN LIFE ALSO MEANS BEING WILLING TO FAIL, over and over again. How do you handle failure? How quickly do you bounce back from adversity?

Failure and defeat can deflate us. Either can feed the little negative voice that lurks inside each one of us, loud and convincing. We start listening to it as it works to undermine our confidence with fabrications such as, "You didn't get the result because you're not good enough or smart enough." The truth is, champions have learned to tune out the negative voice and instead cultivate their empowering voice, the one that says things like "What can I learn from this?," "How can I apply this lesson so that I might benefit from it?" and "What are the advantages of this present situation?"

The secret of resilience will help you persevere in spite of adversity. Here are three summary points you'll read about in these next stories:

1) Stop defining yourself by your setbacks.
2) Become more steadfast in your beliefs to help you remain committed to your goals and to reaching your ultimate destination—a winning life!
3) Have a clear purpose in life to carry you through the most trying of times.

When you're able to learn from your mistakes, adapt your approach, and keep moving forward, you'll have mastered the skill!

There are three steps to becoming more resilient. The first, and most difficult step, is to *believe* in yourself and your goal. Our beliefs are really at the core of who we are. They are designed, in part, to keep us safe. Sometimes it's necessary to let go of our beliefs in order to grow, to increase our awareness, and to embrace new possibilities. We always

Three steps to becoming more resilient:
1. Believe in yourself and your goal;
2. Embrace your bounce back factor;
3. Become what you most desire.

need to be revisiting and reviewing our beliefs so we can better determine which ones are no longer serving us well, and make room for something that will. I call this 'letting go of our disabling beliefs and embracing our empowering beliefs.' Having a clear vision of our goals is an important factor in this first step. A clear vision helps us focus on our major goals and it enhances our resilience and ability to focus on the longer term.

The second step to becoming more resilient is to embrace your own *bounce back factor*, the old 'get back up on the horse' philosophy. Studies have shown that high achievers suffer the same number of setbacks as everybody else. The difference is that the high achievers just bounce back from adversity more quickly.

The third step to becoming more resilient is to *become* what you most desire. Have you ever heard the phrase, "to become a champion you must act like a champion"? It comes back to our basic belief in self. How you believe in yourself, what you believe about yourself, and how you act when you suffer both setbacks and successes are all critical. Master the secret of resiliency and you'll learn to recognize and overcome the little voice in your head that whispers negative, defeating thoughts. Stop being a victim to negative and defeating. You can learn to let go of your limiting beliefs and embrace empowering beliefs.

I've failed more times than I can remember, but along the way I've learned to take my mistakes in stride, laugh a little, and have fun.

By mastering the secret of becoming more resilient you will become unstoppable! As you learn to reframe your failures and adapt your actions to be more effective, you will reach your finish line and achieve your goals in less time. As you read the following five stories, in which I share some of the many setbacks I have had and the lessons I have learned as a result, I encourage you to think about your own resiliency factor. I invite you to consider working with my methods for improving your own resiliency. With a little effort and focus, and a willingness to make mistakes, I'm confident that you will be able to adapt the principles I've offered so that they work for you.

4.1

The Resilience Factor

How Mastering Resilience Will Change Your Life

Picture this: the starting gate for the downhill event at the XVII Winter Olympic Games in Lillehammer, Norway. I stepped into the gate and heard the crowd cheer. This was my event—it was my best chance to win an Olympic medal. I had been training and working towards this day for almost 20 years. It was my opportunity to shine in front of the world.

There were an estimated 50,000 spectators on site, and another 50 million television viewers watching worldwide, all ready to witness the greatest day of my life. I knew that I could win a medal. I had achieved a podium finish in the World Cup Downhill in Saalbach, Austria, three weeks earlier. I had beaten the same roster of skiers just weeks before and I was the gold medal favorite for the event.

As I breathed deeply to both relax and oxygenate my body, I heard the start official say, "10 seconds." I took my position in the gate. The starter shouted, "Racer ready, Go!" I thrust out of the gate and pushed and skated to achieve as much momentum as possible. A quick turn to the right and then to the left. As I cut in on the big right-hand turn, the tails of my skis slide a bit unexpectedly, but I recovered and was back in line. Another turn to the left and then off the second flight, I sailed 35 yards. As I landed, I cut in tight just as I had planned, tighter than any of my competitors, and I made the best turn of my life. I felt the acceleration and speed carry me out of the turn and onto flatter terrain. In my tuck, I flattened my skis for optimal speed and reduced friction, and then, off the big jump—I sailed 75 yards.

As I started the critical left-hand turn, I lost my focus for a split second and, in that instant, I found myself suddenly heading backwards at 85 miles per hour! I careened into the safety net. My mind was screaming, "Nooooooo! No! No! This is not the way it ends. I'm supposed to be on the podium, receiving the gold medal. This is not the ending I imagined. No! All of the training, all of the sweat, the tears, the sacrifices cannot be for this!"

I saw my coach running down the hill towards me with his ski boots on. He looked frantic and was clearly wondering if I was okay. It was all I could do to lift my arm and wave that I was okay, at least physically. Emotionally, I was deeply wounded, feeling as if a truck has just run over me. Twice!

Two volunteers showed up to help me out of the way and I realized that I must move off the course because the competition had to continue. I climbed out of the net and dusted myself off. One of the volunteers handed me a ski that had popped off in the crash. I put my ski back on and crossed the course to a safe place to stand so that the race could resume. I stood there, leaning on my poles, as Kjetl Andre Aamodt from Norway raced past me on his way to a silver medal. I heard the crowd cheer with excitement, cheering for him.

I side slipped down to the bottom of the course and found myself in the finish area. The crowd gave me a cheer. A cheer because I was healthy after the crash, a cheer of sympathy, but not the cheer I had strived for. In a mental fog of dismay and disbelief, I watched as Tommy Moe from the USA won the Gold Medal and teammate Edi Podivinsky from Canada won the bronze. I was excited for my friends, Tommy, Edi, and Kjetil, to witness them have their dreams come true. I smiled for them, as I cried for myself inside.

As a show of respect for the other athletes, I attended the medal awards ceremony that evening. I watched the winners step onto the podium in front of the world and receive their Olympic medals. "Why not me?" I asked myself. I kept thinking, "I worked my ass off for this and yet they get to win! I worked much harder in training than any of them. This isn't fair." I forced myself to watch anyway. I told myself, "Feel the pain. Remember this pain. You don't want to feel this pain again." While I felt entirely deflated, there was a still, small voice within me that said, very quietly, "Not today, not here, but someday, someday it'll be your turn." At that precise moment, I was not ready to hear that still, small voice inside me.

Later the same night, I woke up for a 3:00 AM bathroom visit. It suddenly hit me that it wasn't a bad dream; it actually happened. I just lost my chance to win an Olympic gold medal. I blew it. I crashed and finished the race in the net. Tears welled up and burst through as I sat sobbing on a cold toilet, in the dark, deep within the Olympic Village. How could I give it everything and come up short? I let the tears flow for a few more minutes and then headed back to bed and a fitful sleep.

A week after the fateful Olympic downhill run and my lost opportunity for a gold medal, I was still caught up in the experience. Even though a week had passed since I hoisted my body up from the crash and made my way to the bottom of the mountain, a part of me was still caught up in the net in which I landed on the day of the race. I kept replaying the race over and over again in my mind, ripping myself apart again and again. As I thought about how I missed my chance for victory, I felt absolutely devastated. None of my past achievements before this race seemed to matter. I felt like I had missed the best shot of my career and that it was all over. My spirit and my mind were still caught up in the hard, orange plastic netting. A part of me wondered, "maybe it is just easier to stay in the net." I found myself holding back during training, not skiing to my full potential. I had a horrible realization; I had become "the skier who crashed in the Olympic downhill—the one who blew it." Is this really how I wished to be defined?

Suddenly, that small voice inside me was growing stronger and said, "Okay that's long enough. You've cried, you've moped and you've wallowed in your sorrow and disappointment. If you stay in that net, you will never win. You can choose to continue to mope or you can choose to leave that crash behind you." I realized that I could choose to allow the moment to forever define me or be developed by it. This energizing voice inside me got louder, saying, "You can learn a lesson from this crash, and get back into a winning mindset where you're able to excel. What did you learn? You just need to keep your focus on the task at hand and on your techniques all the

> I realized that I could choose to allow the moment to forever define me or be developed by it.

way down the mountain. You can do it!" I remembered that I was at the top of my game. I started to put things back into a winning perspective, realizing that this was only one race and I had trained my entire life to be the champion that I was now. This wasn't the first race I had lost. I had been conditioned to get back up again, no matter how great the setback. I was surprised by feelings of excitement over the forthcoming race. I decided to get back out there and go for the gold!

A week later, I stepped into the start gate at Aspen, Colorado for the World Cup downhill competition. My concentration was on one race and one race only; right here, right now. I had used what happened at the Olympics two weeks ago to be even more focused this time around. I blasted out of the start gate giving it 100%; I was holding nothing back. I crossed the finish line knowing that I had given it my all and that I completed a fantastic race. After all of the competitors had finished, I was crowned "World Cup Champion." At this moment, I was the best in the world; this is the result I had been striving for my entire life.

When I won the World Cup Championship, it was a phenomenal victory. As I look back now at this period in my athletic career, I realize that had I remained stuck in the net at the Olympics for very much longer—mentally and emotionally speaking—then likely I never would have won a World Cup. I was in peak physical condition at that point in my career. As disheartening as my Olympic performance proved to be, I also knew that I could not afford to take any time away from training or competing. If I was going to become a world champion, this was my time to do so. I had first to grant myself permission to mourn the loss I experienced at the Olympics. I also had to forgive myself for what happened. Finally, I had to decide that I would not be defined by my performance in that race.

Whether or not the net is one for safety purposes on the side of a ski run, we all crash and get caught up in nets from time to time—in relationships, financially, or when we lose an important sale or a valued client. The longer and harder we have worked towards a goal which we subsequently fail to reach, the deeper the potential net we can get caught up in, and the harder it is to get out of that net. As devastated as we are, we need to pick ourselves up, climb out of the net and again pursue our goals wholeheartedly. When we get caught up in a net, we can feel so far away from our next victory. Sometimes our greatest victory can be right around the next corner. For me, it was the very next race.

We must find ways to extricate ourselves from the nets of defeat and learn from our setbacks as opposed to allowing them to deflate and define us.

Victory could be yours with the very next phone call, your very next meeting, or your very next date. We must find ways to extricate ourselves from the nets of defeat and learn from our setbacks as opposed to allowing them to deflate and define us. It is possible to use the pain of our disappointments to refuel our passion to achieve our goals.

In the book, *The Resilience Factor*, by Drs. Karen Reivich and Andrew Shatte, these researchers found that the key defining characteristic among top producers was not that they got knocked down less often than others, but that they got back up more quickly. They had what these authors called the "Resilience Factor." As a professional athlete and ski racer, the reality is that you lose a lot more races than you win. If you want to stay in the game, you have no choice but to learn how to get back up after every defeat. Learning to be resilient is one of the advantages professional athletes can bring to their subsequent endeavors. Resiliency is something that has served me well in many other areas of my life.

As I think about the nets I have got caught up in and climbed out of during my life, I wonder about the nets others get caught up in. Perhaps one of your nets was the hoped-for promotion at work that went to someone else. You

The key defining characteristic among top producers was not that they got knocked down less often than others, but that they got back up more quickly.

may have felt like you had lost your best chance for moving through the ranks of the company. In being passed over for the promotion, you may have believed that you would never be successful in your career. Worse, you may have begun to act as if you were unsuccessful in your career. Then the negative mindset can become a self-fulfilling prophecy. Perhaps the net came in the form of the breakup of a marriage, which caused you to start defining yourself as someone who "fails at relationships." At the time, it may have felt like you would never be in a happy, healthy relationship. Heck, you may even be caught in a net today.

It can be helpful, perhaps even empowering, to know when we are stuck in the net. It is just as important and equally empowering to connect with what has helped us free ourselves from past nets. When we are able to get in touch with whatever it is that motivates us and keeps us striving towards our goals, we are able to bounce back more quickly. It pays to be able to recognize when we are stuck. It pays to know how to bounce back. To connect with your own resilience factor, I invite you to think about the following questions. "Reflect on your life and describe the circumstances and nature of a significant net in which you got caught." Then, think about answering these questions: "What motivated you?, What kept you striving for your goal/s?, What were the core drivers in your life? What helped you to get out of that net?"

If you are able to identify what has helped you to be resilient in the past, this knowledge can become a lifelong resource you can tap into, time and again, as an aid to overcoming the challenges you face in your life today. Connect with your inner resilience to uncover the champion inside you!

4.2

Who's To Blame When You're Not Winning?

How A Hit On The Head Helped Me Move From Victimhood To Victory

I stood over my desk, watching my tears fall onto the open phone book in front of me, creating dark wet splotches that wrinkled and bound the thin pages together. I felt utterly defeated.

You see, I could not find the phone number I was looking for because I could not find the name I was looking for. What was getting in my way was that I no longer remembered the alphabet.

Not remembering the alphabet was only the tip of what I had been experiencing. For about two and a half months, I had been unable to read for more than a minute or walk more than a block and a half without feeling dizzy.

For much of my life, my sole focus had been to become a World Cup downhill skiing champion—longing to get just three-tenths of a second faster. Now all I could think about was, "would I ever be normal again, as incredible as normal can seem to be when you feel unwell?"

You must be wondering what happened to move me from world-class athlete to living like a 95-year-old man. Worry not, I will share this fascinating part of my story with you. I'll also share what I discovered about winning during a long period of convalescence—some eight and a half months in all—and how you can use this knowledge to achieve better results for yourself.

So what happened? I was racing in the World Cup downhill event in Beaver Creek, Colorado when something took place that would forever change my life in the most extraordinary way.

I had virtually completed the World Cup race and my split time put me in first position; I entered the last turn on the course with too much speed for the line I had picked. I hit a small bump I neglected to see on the inspection run and was suddenly knocked off balance. Still trying to recover a split second later, I hit the finishing jump at a speed of 85 miles per hour (135 kilometres per hour) and launched 15 feet into the air, sailing directly sideways.

This would be akin to jumping off the top of a semi-trailer truck that is traveling far above the speed limit on a snowy highway.

All I could think was, "Can I land this?" There are split seconds just before a crash, when time seems to expand and events slow down from fractions of a second to slow motion to a complete stop. I'm all too familiar with the phrase "my life flashed in front of my eyes." If you've ever been in an accident where you recognized the inevitability of the accident before the actual event, you'll know what I mean.

The next thing I remember was waking up in an ambulance. I asked, "Where am I?" A paramedic responded, "You're in an ambulance and we're on our way to the hospital in Vail." Completely disoriented, I asked, "Really, what happened?" The paramedic gently explained to me, "Well you were in a ski race today." I was amazed. Not having any idea what had just happened, I innocently asked, "Really, I was in a race? How did I do?"

Over the days that passed, I discovered not only my results in the race, but the consequences of my crash—a severe concussion. I was told I was lucky to be alive. Three days after being released from the hospital, I boarded a plane to fly home.

I had a crooked neck, one eye closed to compensate for the double vision, and scars down my face. My parents came to the airport to greet me. I looked at my mom and said, "Don't worry Mom, I'll be ready to race again in three days."

I wasn't ready in three days. Back at home, I was told that there was no way of knowing how long a concussion might last. Even worse, I was informed that there was nothing that could be done to help the healing process and that all I could do would be to rest and wait it out. The main problem for me, given this wait-and-see prescription, was that the XVIII Winter Olympic Games in Nagano, Japan were coming up in just two short months.

I paid attention to the medical advice—to wait it out—for about 24 hours before I did the exact opposite and moved into action. I tried everything I could think of. I met with neurologists, underwent CAT and MRI scans, I sought out cranial massage therapy and chiropractic care. I even went as far as shaving my head so I could have round-the-clock acupuncture treatments.

Days turned into weeks, and weeks into months, as I experimented with different treatments. All the while, I remained in a state of almost complete mental and physical collapse.

My head had become a giant stress-o-meter. Fielding a business call, reading for more than a minute, or sitting on the toilet would cause my head to throb such that I would need to lie down to recover for over an hour. I had little decision-making capacity, zero energy, and absolutely no short-term memory.

As time passed I remained unfit for training. I began to wonder whether I would be assessed as sufficiently fit and healthy to compete in the Nagano Winter Olympic Games. With each passing day, I became more frustrated and impatient with my situation. I began to pity myself, wondering and asking, "Why did this happen to me?"

I became quite depressed. It became harder and harder to wake up every day and continue to search for solutions.

Venturing outside into the world beyond my home and bedroom was how I imagined a walk down the strip in Las Vegas might be like while listening to heavy metal music, full volume, on headphones. My head simply ached. I needed to find a way to stop the world from spinning so I could experience some relief, if only for a little while.

I needed to stop listening to what everyone else thought I should do to heal myself and instead find a place of stillness where I could look inside for the answers. The place I found was something like a poor man's sensory deprivation tank and it became my sanctuary. It was the walk-in closet in my bedroom, which was both quiet and dark, once the door was closed. What I found within this sanctuary was a voice that changed my life forever.

I don't know if you have ever put yourself in a similarly low stimulus environment; when it's dark, and quiet, your mind just races. After three days of lying still in that closet, in a moment of humility, I asked, rather, I begged, "Please God, please let me get better so that I can win the gold medal." A voice inside me said, "There are lots of people who want to win, why should you? What good are you going to do with it?"

A voice within me started to channel the good that I would do if I won. In the closet, I wrote down brief notes about my thoughts, hoping that I would be able to read and still make sense of them later.

In answering that question, I became free. Somehow I had found a new energy and my first feeling of some simultaneous Ah Ha's that would change the course of my life. In that moment I was changed. By finally looking beyond the victory and for the good that I could do, I found inspiration. Motivation takes energy, but inspiration can carry us. When I stopped looking to the medical experts to provide me with solutions, I was able to turn inward and find some measure of peace with my present situation. I found inspiration in a calling that lay beyond the finish line of a World Cup victory.

Unfortunately, I did miss my opportunity to compete in the XVII Winter Olympic Games in 1998, in Nagano, Japan, yet I was newly inspired to assume the challenge ahead of me and keep looking for solutions so I might return to World Cup competition and, perhaps, participate in the subsequent Winter Olympic Games in 2002, which were to be hosted in the US, in Salt Lake City.

The internal, spiritual therapy I experienced in the closet ultimately provided me with an opportunity to find the right external support. After eight and a half months of living a severely restricted life, I very quickly found the solution after a spur-of-the-moment decision I made to fly to Colorado Springs.

On the advice of a teammate, I flew to Colorado Springs to see Dr. Michael Leahy for a consultation and assessment for a procedure called Active Release Techniques (ART). Dr. Leahy performed a massage-like maneuver on my neck that took about two minutes and released a muscle that had, according to him, adhered to the brain stem. In doing so, it was as if he had flipped a switch and given me my life back; I very rapidly experienced a complete mental and physical recovery.

Before the concussion, whenever I had been faced with a challenge or a setback, I always expressed some doubt in my ability to bounce back, wondering, "Can I make it through this? Can I recover?" Now I know that the answer is always going to be yes, so long as I am connected with a true purpose. Being clear about our higher purpose in life gives us the conviction we need to make it through the toughest of times by affirming for us our worthiness to win.

If we do not connect with our higher purpose, it is too easy to wallow in self-pity and depression. Perhaps worse, we can get stuck in neutral asking useless questions like, "Why me?" I have never found a solution to any problem situation when I asked that question.

> *Being clear about our higher purpose in life gives us the conviction we need to make it through the toughest of times by affirming for us our worthiness to win.*

Instead, when we connect with our higher purpose and the good we can do, we discover an inner strength greater than we could ever have previously imagined. We realize that we have the power to create the reality that we desire. We stop looking outside for the answers and instead find peace in searching our inner landscape.

Has anything ever happened to you where you have found yourself stuck, repeatedly asking, "Why me?" Do you ever have a feeling of being unmotivated or frustrated with your current situation? Have you ever found yourself looking outside to experts to provide you with a solution instead of turning inward in search of some peace over your present circumstances? If you can achieve this sense of peace, my experience tells me that enlightenment can follow. Are you clear about your higher purpose in life?

I encourage you to write down your answer to the same question I asked myself, "What good will you do when you do win?" Think about some of the goals you have established for yourself.

If you can achieve the goals you have envisioned for yourself, what will you then do for the greater good? You will be amazed by the power of this process! Trust me, and trust yourself.

> *If you can achieve the goals you have envisioned for yourself, what will you then do for the greater good?*

Notes To Yourself

4.3

The Faster You're Going, The Further Ahead You Need To Look!

The Power In Having A Long Term Vision

My alarm went off at 7:00 AM for the fourth morning in a row. I felt tired and wanted to sleep longer. I was sleeping eight hours a night, yet it didn't seem like enough. (A few years later, I discovered that I could function effectively on only four or five hours of sleep).

I just wasn't as engaged in my work and felt fatigued. I didn't know what was wrong. I'm typically extremely engaged and excited about work, especially so when I've been reaching my goals; yet, it felt as though something was missing. I wasn't feeling as excited about what I was doing or about where I was going, at least not as excited as I knew I would like to be. Yet, I couldn't seem to identify and put my finger on what was missing.

About a week later, I received some valuable insight from my business and financial coach. His principle point in our session together had been to emphasize that most people live life being far too shortsighted and plan ahead only year-to-year. They can get really clear about what they want to accomplish for the year ahead and then focus on that year, with a just-in-time planning paradigm. He suggested I get crystal clear on my ten-year vision and, if I could accomplish that, I would achieve much more over the coming year than I would ever do if I just focused on that same year alone. I realized I had, for the past year at least, allowed my focus to narrow, looking just one year ahead. I had certainly spent time looking further ahead than the next twelve months, but I had not really crystallized or shared my long-term vision with anyone else.

> *Get crystal clear on your ten-year vision and, if you can accomplish that, you will achieve much more over the coming year than ever you will do if you focus on that same year alone.*

115

Even though I coach other people in this same process of crystallizing their vision and naming their "big worthy target," I had been over-looking the process for myself. Perhaps my own short-sightedness lay in the fact I had established a five year "big worthy target," and had recently achieved it. You might be thinking, "Well what's the matter with that?" I had accomplished what I had set out to do, and simply hadn't set a new, long-term target. Indeed, I had not established another five-year target and had been cruising; instead settling for a gentle improvement based on the same target. I had fallen into a trap of being shortsighted and settling for, primarily, short-term results. I had become caught in what I call the "breadcrumb trap," or "myopia trap," wherein I was only looking far enough ahead to deal with the next thing, instead of looking at the big picture and even farther ahead.

In ski racing, we had a saying, "The faster you're going, the further ahead you need to look." It is absolutely true! In ski racing, when I wasn't looking far enough ahead, I would be forced into reacting immediately. Not only would this make for a rough ride, my timing, inevitably, would also be a bit too late. It felt like I was going way too fast because I was just bouncing and reacting; in reality, I was actually skiing more slowly. Conversely, when I looked further ahead, I would see things sooner and be able to anticipate more and react at the appropriate time, in accordance with the conditions. All of this makes for a smoother ride and a better result. When I practiced this, my runs always felt slower but smoother and I was able to achieve faster descents. No doubt about it, looking further down the hill made for better results.

Similarly, in the business world, not looking far enough ahead put me into a more defensive mode of reaction; it seemed as if everything was coming at me too quickly to react appropriately. With no new and clearly stated target, I became unfocused. Furthermore, I simply wasn't as energized when I attempted to move forward with only a short-term vision.

I have a great deal to learn about achievement, but one of the most powerful lessons I learned from sport is to keep striving for better results by implementing good ideas, which is really my definition of "being coachable." The next gift to myself was to find and hire two well-respected facilitators to work with me and help guide me through a 12-year visioning exercise. We took a couple of extra days to break the 12-year period into more detailed six year, four year, two year,

> One of the most powerful lessons I learned from sport is to keep striving for better results by implementing good ideas, which is really my definition of "being coachable."

one year, Q1 to Q4, monthly, and daily plans and targets. Let me tell you, I found this a tough exercise to work through. It took a considerable amount of energy both from my facilitators and myself.

It will probably not be a surprise to you to hear that we have already accomplished more in the last two months of business than we accomplished during the previous six months. My facilitation team and I are crystal clear about my goals and have established timeframes and measurable targets for their achievement. Defining these interim goals was only possible by becoming crystal clear on the 12-year vision. In addition, I have established and reached new personal fitness goals and my family unit is as strong as it has ever been. The most pleasant surprise to me has been the change in my excitement level about every single day. I feel more fully engaged in what I am doing because my efforts are now connected with a greater purpose.

This long-term visioning exercise is completely congruent with my experiences in professional sport and with how as a six-year-old child I visualized myself crossing the finish line to win a World Cup downhill event. It took me two decades to finally, and fortunately, see that dream come true. Like so many lessons in life, I had intuitively known the power of long-term visioning from a very early age, but I had neglected the process and stopped practicing the exercise of vividly picturing my future that far in advance.

As I've mentioned, I had stopped looking at the big picture and far enough ahead to the future. When I consider the mantra from ski racing, "The faster you're going, the further ahead you need to look," I know that it is true. What has been more powerful for me though is the realization that, "the further ahead we look, the faster we go." I do not mean this in the sense of feeling like we're moving faster but we're actually going quite slowly. No, this kind of going fast is about speed that feels natural and at ease, and still allows us to reach our mileposts and achieve consistent, solid results. Not only do we achieve our goals more quickly, we find clarity, energy, passion and purpose in our pursuit.

I am so happy to be able to have so many smart and successful people in my life who coach and support me, both with new knowledge and occasionally, to remind me of things that I have always known and sometimes forget. With my 12-year vision crystallized, I am excited, passionate, and in love with the process of helping people live their "winning life."

If you are at all like me, I'm sure that there are areas in your life where you may want to gain some additional momentum. The best way I know to achieve that momentum is to be crystal clear about your long-term vision. Are you laser focused 10 to 15 years ahead? To achieve more in the next year than you ever thought possible, write a paragraph (or two, or twenty) about your 10- to 15-year vision. Color it in with details. Where do you see yourself? Who else is there? What do you want to achieve, be, do, have and see? Design and develop a rich picture in your mind and color it with as many of the fine points as you can. Once you have this vision in your mind, share it with someone so it comes alive.

4.4

Make Everything You Touch Turn To Gold!

Learn How Everything Can Be Used To Your Advantage

Focus!

As the clock ticked down to the start of the World Cup Downhill ski race in Sierra Nevada, Spain, I knew I was ready. Not merely ready in the sense of, "I've got my skis and goggles on, and I'm not burdened with any injuries." No, I mean really ready! I'd never felt so ready for anything in my entire life.

I'd trained all year for this race. I was at the peak of my form. I'd had the perfect amount of sleep the night before. I'd eaten the perfect meal at precisely the right time. My muscles felt warm and limber. I was psyched-up. By the time I was heading for the start line, only 100 feet away, I was in the zone, primed to shoot down the course when the clock counted down.

Then an announcement over the public address system stopped me dead in my tracks:

"All downhill race competitors please return to the lodge."

What?

"The race has been delayed due to a heavy tailwind."

Delayed?

"We'll update you in two hours time and confirm whether the race will go ahead or not."

Hey, whoa, hold on a second! I trained all year for this and now you're telling me it might not even go ahead? You do this to me now, less than a minute before start-time? What the heck is going on?

Anyone up close could have seen the condensation in my breath in the cold air of the mountains, but I swear, right then, you could probably have seen steam coming right out of my ears! I was rumbling like a volcano. When I got back to the lodge, I saw I wasn't alone; a lot of my competitors were slamming their helmets on the floor and pounding their fists on the tables. Everyone was furious, complaining loudly—and I joined right in with the rest of them.

Angry comments flew around the room. "Every damn race this season has been delayed. Who the heck's in charge here?" "Why wait till the last minute? There was no tailwind an hour ago, but now there is?" "These guys haven't got a clue what they're doing!"

And so it went for the next 10 or 15 minutes; a whole group of frustrated skiers ranting and raving amongst themselves. We listed all the different ways that the officials had screwed up and all the reasons why they should be fired. I was explaining to anyone standing around and willing to listen how the officials really ought to be running the event. Every so often, I tossed in a question like, "How would they like it if …?" and "What do they take us for …?"

I'd like to say it felt good, the chance to let off some steam. However, the longer I continued with my ranting, the more frustrated I felt. After all, nothing was actually changing. No matter how much we complained, the race wasn't going to start any sooner. Eventually, I realized what was going on and that what I was participating in was really all about negative thinking, and it wasn't helping.

I stopped talking for a while, took some deep breaths and reminded myself of a belief I had lately been consciously working with, and I said to myself: "This situation could be to my advantage if I can figure out how to make it to my advantage." That simple statement and self-talk helped me turn a corner and redirect my energies. Immediately, my brain responded with the question: "OK, so how can this situation be to my advantage?"

Now that I'd led my thoughts in a particular direction, the cogs started turning and my brain was off and running: "Well, if there's a heavy tailwind now, it's fair to assume there will still be a moderate tailwind at race time. If that turns out to be true, the course is going to run faster, which means I'm going to have more speed than during the training runs. I'll need more courage and quicker reaction times. If I can spend the time remaining before my new start time in visualizing the course running faster and with slightly quicker timing and quicker reactions, then I can turn this delay to my advantage."

And that's exactly what I did. For most of the remaining hour and 45 minutes, I pictured myself on the course. I felt the tailwind pushing me forward, I saw myself starting the turns a little sooner, coming into the jumps a little faster and not tucking in so much because I had a tailwind. When the race eventually got underway, I skied well, and achieved a new personal record at the time. I came 7th in the World Cup, my first top ten placing. I had reached a new level of performance.

What had happened? I had committed to using a constructive belief that the delay could be turned to my advantage—if only I could figure out how. That realization prompted the simple question, "How is this delay to my advantage?" And that question led me to the idea of visualizing the course with a tailwind and recording a new personal best.

Not everyone committed to the same belief. At the finish line, some of my competitors were saying, "I blew it, that race came at me faster today, my timing was off, I made all kinds of mistakes … ." The reactions and responses of many of my peers simply reinforced for me how important it is to condition our beliefs for success.

When I look at the state I was in before I decided to discipline my thoughts and beliefs, I was caught in a negative cycle of asking pointless questions, of casting blame, and complaining about things I couldn't control. That mindset simply sent me off on a whirlwind of unhelpful thoughts and damaging emotions, causing me unnecessary stress.

To be honest, sometimes it's easy for me to allow myself to be sucked in to the negativity created by other people, especially when I'm feeling frustrated. That's why my first response to the delay was to join in the hullabaloo, get all stressed out, and ask a lot of heated questions that led me nowhere useful. I remember the day because I learned how we can turn a curveball into an advantage. After all, change is inevitable, and we will always need to be able to adapt.

If we are to become truly adaptive in the face of change, we can't always rely on our natural predispositions, or our habitual way of thinking. To do so isn't always going to be optimal thinking. My own initial thinking certainly wasn't optimal that day in

> *If we are to become truly adaptive in the face of change, we can't always rely on our natural predispositions, or our habitual way of thinking. To do so isn't always going to be optimal thinking.*

> *To succeed and make success sustainable, there's no other way, we have to learn to "drive" our brain as much as possible, instead of letting it run on autopilot and letting our limiting thoughts take over.*

Sierra Nevada, Spain, and it often still isn't. I work on my beliefs constantly. To succeed and make success sustainable, there's no other way, we have to learn to "drive" our brain as much as possible, instead of letting it run on autopilot and letting our limiting thoughts take over.

The key to reacting to change in a positive way is to better train our beliefs beforehand. Had I done that, when the race was delayed, I would have more quickly asked, "How can I turn this situation to my advantage?" As soon as you ask yourself a constructive question, you're more likely to come up with a constructive answer. I did! I visualized the course with a tailwind and skied the race of my life.

> *As soon as you ask yourself a constructive question, you're more likely to come up with a constructive answer.*

What are your own limiting beliefs? Have you ever been caught in a whirlwind of destructive thinking and negative emotions? Have you found yourself asking destructive questions and thinking destructive thoughts about money, success, change, new circumstances, or other people? If so, it may be time to challenge some of your beliefs.

Take time to examine your beliefs about money, success, relationships, setbacks, other people, and your own potential. Such beliefs are fundamental and will influence your ability to win. Over the next two weeks, whenever you're faced with a challenge, consider repeating this mantra: "This challenge is to my advantage if I can figure out how to make it to my advantage."

And then ask yourself the question: "How is this to my advantage?" Believing that everything that happens, good or not, can be used to fuel our success is another step towards achieving success ... and happiness.

4.5

84-Year-Old Woman Dies From Eating Horse

The Crazy Things People Will Do To Avoid Looking Stupid

My mother was and is a great mother and she is also an outstanding grandmother. One day, she was teaching my son Colby the song about an old lady who swallowed a fly.

I couldn't recall this particular song from my own childhood but, as I listened to it now, I wondered how dumb could the old lady be if she swallowed a spider in the hope that it would eat the fly that she also just swallowed. For those of you who know the song, the old lady then swallows a bird to get the spider. She goes on to swallow many other things before swallowing a horse—something which is to her ultimate undoing and demise.

As I was thinking, "What a dumb old lady," a realization hit me like a kick in the chest from the old lady's horse. "Yikes," I thought, "I have eaten a menagerie of insects and farm animals myself."

A few years ago, a salesman my family knew, we'll call him Rick, was starting a new company. He was looking for financial backing for his new venture. I listened to his sales pitch and decided to invest, both to help out Rick and because it sounded like a good business plan. I made an initial investment of $30,000 in Rick's project.

Four months later, Rick reported expenses were higher than he had anticipated and sales had been lower than projected. He asked me for another $20,000 without which he might have to resort to closing the enterprise down. I obliged, but put a lien on his property to secure the $20,000.

Another year went by and times remained tough for Rick. This time he told me, "If you can't loan me another $7,500, I'm going to have to close the doors." While I was skeptical, it seemed prudent to give him the $7,500 to protect the $50,000 I had already invested. Then the inevitable happened and Rick's business finally went under.

Rick then hatched a plan to earn back my investment in him, and fast. His plan was to subdivide the 20 acres of land he owned and sell it to a property developer.

This is where my salivary glands for big farm animals started to kick in. Rick's partner in the property would sell his third and I could buy this share. I'd then be a legitimate owner of one-third of the property, my name would be on the title, and I'd share in both the profits from the land sale and be reimbursed for the $57,500 I'd invested with Rick in his now-defunct business venture.

If you've been following this little story closely, you're probably thinking that my willingness to pursue further business dealings with Rick would be foolhardy, and you would be right.

While I deliberated over the land sale and development investment long and hard before making a decision, I agreed to participate because it seemed I would see the return of my earlier $57,500 investment more promptly. I extended a further $50,000 to Rick—yes, you read that correctly, a further $50,000—to become a one-third owner of the 20-acre parcel and set to work to obtain the development approved.

Wouldn't you know it, Rick's luck just got worse, and pretty soon I was in receipt of a letter from a lawyer which stated the bank was going to foreclose on the property. Apparently, Rick had not been paying the mortgage or taxes on the property, nor even the monthly minimums on his credit card accounts. Suddenly, I realized that my name was now on the property title and my credit rating was receiving a black eye because of the situation.

I jumped in with both feet and brought the mortgage payments up to date but just as quickly realized that I couldn't carry the expense indefinitely. I tried to negotiate with Rick to turn the property over to me but he refused. Finally, before the bank foreclosed, but not soon enough to avoid about $30,000 in legal fees, along with a good deal of stress and many a sleepless night, Rick signed the property over to me. However, unfortunately for me, the way the deal was structured meant Rick would still share in the profits of the sale of the property once it was subdivided.

To date, I estimate I have spent more on the property than it is worth and have a significant mortgage to cover. Rick is still living in the only house on the property, which he has agreed to pay rent, but has yet to do so. Given the legal situation and local bylaws, I'm not at liberty to evict him, even though I have never received any rental income.

This saga is not yet over. Rick is still trying to have the subdivision of the property approved and so we remain reluctant business partners for now.

In hindsight, I realize I swallowed a fly, then a spider, then a bird, and likely a cat and a dog as well. I am bound and determined not to swallow the horse by investing another dime in what has become the proverbial sinking ship.

When I think about the concept of the old lady swallowing the fly, I'm embarrassed to admit that I've swallowed a few myself. For a further example, before I met and married Kristina, I was in a long-term relationship that was not working particularly well. Instead of cutting my losses, I just kept trying harder to make the relationship work. I did this even after my gut instinct told me the relationship was doomed. I continued to invest time and energy in the relationship, thereby swallowing the fly, the spider, the bird, and the cat!

I have also seen others fall victim to this pattern of making unwise investments. My brother-in-law purchased a film-processing laboratory at a time of considerable upheaval in a rapidly changing industry. Rather than recognize his mistake promptly, he purchased more expensive equipment and obtained a bigger business loan. He swallowed the spider.

I was laughing about my own mistakes with my friend Jordy, who happens to be a psychologist. Jordy told me that there is actually a fancy name for this phenomenon, the "sunk cost error." It is this crazy thing that happens when we won't admit to ourselves that we have, in fact, made a

> *It is this crazy thing that happens when we won't admit to ourselves that we have, in fact, made a mistake. In the end, we often compound the original blunder and make everything much worse.*

mistake. Instead of admitting our mistake, we try to undo the original mishap by sinking more money, or more effort, or more time into the

> *Often times, admitting we have made a mistake and cutting our losses is the smartest course of action we can take.*

venture or relationship. In the end, we often compound the original blunder and make everything much worse.

I wonder whether you have been caught by the "sunk cost error" and, if so, how it may have impacted you? Can you recall a time when you tried to avoid learning a life lesson by, metaphorically speaking, tucking a napkin over your shirt as you prepared to eat a whole barnyard of insects and animals? Perhaps this cautionary tale is as poignant for you today as it was for me because you're about to put a forkfull of horse into your mouth in an attempt to avoid admitting to yourself that you've made a mistake?

Where might you need to cut your losses?

5
Teamwork Wins

THIS FINAL SECRET TO WINNING not only makes winning possible, it makes it easier. From all my years in professional sport, I've learned that winning requires teamwork. Sure, you can try to do it all by yourself, but I guarantee that you'll be more successful if you leverage the talents of others.

In this section, I will share stories about how you can work with a team so that you can save time and energy and improve your own results. You will learn how to surround yourself with the right people who can help you to stay motivated and achieve the results you desire. This secret is the last piece of my winning formula, and it is critical to your success.

Before we can understand how to leverage the talent of others, we have to overcome a natural instinct that all human beings seem to possess. The instinct I'm referring to is sometimes called the 'silo mentality,' and it is certainly fostered by our Western culture that promotes and values independence. From time to time, most of us have succumbed to the desire to head back to the security of our own cave (home) to try and resolve our problems all by ourselves. When we don't know the answer to something, it is sometimes difficult for us to admit our shortcomings, because we feel that to do so would confirm our vulnerability and weakness. Instead, we try to learn everything, fix everything, and do everything ourselves. This mindset is natural, but it is certainly not the most beneficial approach to adopt or follow.

Rather than continue trying to achieve everything yourself, consider adopting the idea of having training partners. Training partners are either people who are themselves striving to reach goals similar to your own or are capable of assisting you in some way to achieve your goals. Through working with training partners, you can become aware of new knowledge that is critical to your success. With the right training partners, not only should you receive honest feedback, you will benefit by seeing problems and solutions from a different and valued perspective.

Training partners can provide support in many areas of your life. In professional sports, we had coaches and physical therapists looking after us, but members of the ski team also paired up so each of us had a dedicated training partner who helped push us to improve our physical performance. We had other support from dieticians and nutritionists, and of course our coaches and physical therapists also made sure we were not pushing ourselves too far or too soon. Through healthy competition, our teammates also helped each of us see what we were capable of achieving.

In my experience, training partners can help us know when to stop procrastinating and start taking action. Training partners can show us how to sustain our motivation by staying focused on our performance instead of letting our attention wander in directions that do nothing to increase the quality of our results. Training partners can also help us to be persistent. When we are struggling through a difficult period in our life, we often do not need to look very far for a training partner who will support us and encourage us to persevere.

Outside of sport, training partners are also commonplace. Financial advisors might be seen as training partners to help us reach our financial goals. Personal coaches can help us achieve our professional goals. Spiritual leaders can help us achieve our personal goals.

By embracing and harnessing the secret of teamwork, we can redefine the process of winning. When it works, teamwork can energize your desire to succeed. It can increase your confidence and clarify your sense of purpose. Teamwork can be inspirational because it offers the opportunity to access the power of reciprocation. You may have heard of the law of attraction. When we are successful in achieving our goals, we are more likely to attract similarly successful people. When we create strategic alliances and training partnerships with other, similarly successful and motivated individuals, we can create a dynamic force.

Winning with the support of others alongside us also feels different. If you're able to harness the dynamic tension that is created between high achievers determined to reach a goal, you will find that you're able to reach your goals more quickly. Sometimes it takes a critical moment to understand the value of learning through others.

There is a dynamic synergy and energy that is created when people join together to achieve a common goal. The energy seems to feed off itself and grow exponentially. Most people are attracted by positive energy and by success. As you experience success, likely you'll find your team will grow, and the right team for you will lead to greater success. The process is dynamic and seems to take on a life of its own. If you've experienced this, then you'll know what I mean. It is a dynamic and wonderful experience. It is so much better to win with a team than to win alone. In fact, I think the good life is really about winning together.

It took a long time and many lessons before I learned to truly value my teammates; before I learned to leverage the strengths of others in order to further my own success. Every day, we are presented with opportunities to grow and become better people. The challenge for each of us is to recognize these opportunities, to recognize and seek out those people from whom we can learn and through whom we can improve ourselves. It is important that we remember and acknowledge the support we receive from all those around us, not just our training partners. For much of my early life, I took for granted the support I received from those people who were closest to me.

> *It is so much better to win with a team than to win alone. In fact, I think the good life is really about winning together.*

Join me as I share some of these personal experiences with you. In mastering the power of teamwork, you will achieve your goals more quickly and derive greater enjoyment in the process. As you read through these stories, I invite you to consider the current members of your team and challenge yourself to learn from them. I also invite you to consider whether there is someone else that you know, whom you could invite to join your team, and who could improve your performance right now.

Notes To Yourself

5.1

Act Now Or Pay Later

The Cost Of Doing Nothing

All my life, I have dedicated myself to the pursuit of my dreams. Becoming a champion ski racer was a dream I pursued from the time I was a small child. Wealth creation is a more recent dream but still one I began pursuing when I was just 20 years old.

The pursuit of wealth creation has really been no different than the pursuit of ski racing. I knew the first step I needed to take was to find a resource to support me. I became interested in real estate as a means of investment and read *Nothing Down for the 90s* by Robert Allen. His concepts seemed solid and I became quite enamoured of the prospects of embarking on my next dream. At the dinner table one evening, I excitedly announced to my parents, "I want to buy a property." They were less than thrilled with this idea.

I sought another opinion, this time from a friend. He was even more skeptical than my parents had been, proclaiming, "Experts don't write books. If they are any good at what they do, they are busy making money doing just that, not sharing their secrets with the world. The so-called experts who write books are just trying to profit from selling a book because they can't make money any other way."

I didn't know whose advice I should listen to. I began to ask myself, "Is the information in Robert Allen's book true? Does the author really know what he is talking about? Is it a scam? Could his strategies actually help me become rich as he claims?" I didn't know whether I should follow the advice in the book and invest in real estate or not.

In the end, it was easier to do nothing. My uncertainty led to inactivity and I didn't buy a property that summer. Given the real estate market that year, likely I lost more than $10,000 as a result of doing nothing. The greater loss, however, was the time lost and the lost opportunity cost of the compounding effect of that $10,000 because I failed to follow through.

By the following summer, I realized the dream of wealth creation had become a serious goal for me, and one that was not going to diminish in spite of my lack of action. I felt ready to take action. I decided to take the plunge and implement the ideas in Allen's book.

I put a down payment on my first property using the $10,000 I had saved. I had to find a partner to purchase it with me because I didn't have sufficient funds for the required down payment and was unable to qualify for a mortgage on my own. One year later, my partner and I sold the property and more than doubled our money. I had learned my lesson about inactivity caused by uncertainty and quickly reinvested my profits. Over the next fifteen years I was fortunate to grow my initial investment a few hundred fold.

When I think back to the year I spent in a state of uncertainty, I realize the importance of decision-making. On many subsequent occasions, I have sought out new insights with a view to improving my life, but have just as often failed to follow through with their implementation. In fact, even when I discover a new idea, and I agree with its potential, I still don't act in my own best interests or act to change anything.

We can be given the keys (presented with the means) but if we don't put them in the lock and turn the knob, we will never open any doors for ourselves. It is possible to become more wealthy, more fit, happier, and build better relationships when we stay open to alternative or innovative ways of thinking and then implement these proven strategies.

> We can be given the keys (presented with the means) but if we don't put them in the lock and turn the knob, we will never open any doors for ourselves.

Once you find strategies that you believe will help you achieve your goals, it is time to act. How many times have you become aware of a great idea, perhaps by reading a book, but have failed to act on your new knowledge. Are you reading for theoretical understanding or for practical application? Are you a know-it-all but implement-a-little? I encourage you to research and learn, but you need to know when it is time to stop researching and begin applying your new knowledge.

Are You Still Focusing On What You Can't Control?

How To Stop Moping And Start Winning

During my career, I won two World Cup Championships. My first victory was in Val Gardena, Italy, for which I never received a trophy. Nobody really recognized I won the race at all.

Let me describe what happened on that occasion, which may explain why everyone overlooked my achievement.

After an amazing race, I checked the scoreboard to see that I was 1.5 seconds ahead of my nearest competitor. In downhill skiing 1.5 seconds represents one heck of a margin! It is the equivalent of winning a 100-yard dash by 10 yards. I was elated and raised my hands in excitement. This result represented my best career performance to date, and I had managed to do it when it mattered, at a World Cup event.

The execution of my performance had felt both like a flow experience and fate—my destiny. The moment was perfect. I felt perfect. It was a dream come true.

I was standing at the finish line, waiting for the results of the remaining competitors and to hear the officials broadcast the final results of the race. The competitor following me posted a time 1.75 seconds slower! I loved the moment—everything about it. The cheers from the crowd, the beauty of the setting, and most of all, the magnitude of my winning margin! After ten further competitors had followed me down the course, I remained more than a second ahead of the next fastest skier. Someone bring the champagne!

My winning time remained unbeaten for a further 20 competitors, but then the announcer suddenly got excited. Apparently someone had bettered me, beating my split time on the upper part of the course. Sure enough, number 30 momentarily moved into first place. By the time he had completed his run, going more slowly down the lower half of the course, his final time put him 0.5 of a second behind me. Whew, that was a little close but I was still in first place. Results change rapidly in downhill skiing, and competitor number 31 finished just 0.25 seconds behind me and moved into second spot on the board. My lead margin was narrowing and each successive skier appeared to be descending the course in a shorter time. By the time the 35th competitor had taken his run, my time had been bested. How could this be?

But wait a second, competitor number 36 just moved into first place. As I stood there, scratching my head, competitor number 37 moved into the lead. I was now in fourth place. What the heck was going on?

I looked around and realized what had been happening. It was the weather! The sun had appeared and on the upper part of the course, the fresh snow that had fallen overnight had probably begun to glaze. Glazed snow is not only faster, it offers skiers a speed advantage the more skis scrape over it. That meant that the course was getting faster and faster for each subsequent skier.

Each competitor continued to better the time of the racer preceding him. Somewhat predictably, one of the last racers, number 66, won the race. It's usually a complete anomaly in downhill racing for such a late racer to win a competition. In fact, it's virtually unheard of. By the time it was all over, I was in 12th place.

I felt sick. I don't have adequate words to fully describe how it feels to move from complete elation to profound disappointment. Emotionally, it's a rollercoaster nightmare. You wish you could run away from the reality, but you can't; you just stay rooted to the spot you're in, head spinning, feeling completely out of control.

I was still reeling over the reversal of fortunes as I watched the winners step up to the podium to receive their trophies. Cameras were flashing and microphones were jostled as the media rushed to interview the new champions. No one cared about me. No one cared that I had just skied the best race of my life.

It all felt so unjust and I let my profound disappointment get the better of me. All my life, I had trained for such a moment as this—to ski my best and achieve what I thought was a winning performance at a World Cup event. Indeed, this is exactly what I had done. I realized then that the real source of my frustration came not from a feeling of being defeated by other skiers, but in being defeated by the weather!

I felt overwhelmingly depressed and withdrew into a silent cocoon. I didn't talk to anyone, not even my service technician, Dave Armstrong, despite his outstanding support. If I could have slipped quietly into an isolation tank for the next 48 hours, I would have done so.

Four days later, it was time to race again, but I was still unbelievably grouchy. The self-righteous, distorted nature of my thoughts ran wild. "They just won because of dumb luck. I'm going to prove to everyone how I should have won the World Cup!" When it was my turn to run the course, I attacked it, more focused on proving myself (and working out my anger) than delivering my best performance. Not surprisingly, I performed so poorly I had no chance of winning, nor even of placing in the top three.

Afterwards, I realized that none of my moping around was helping. In fact, I had allowed my anger and bitterness to undermine my performance ability. I couldn't change what had happened, but I could get my act together. I couldn't afford to lose or post poor results while staying sore about losing a previous race.

Yes, it's unfair that the weather intervened and worked against me after I put in such a good performance. However, if I was honest with myself, I must concede that there have been times when the weather and all the other variable conditions were on my side and gave me the edge. Sometimes, winning can be about the luck of the draw!

The fact is that there will always be variables, like weather, or the economy, which are beyond our immediate control. All you can ever do, or give, is your best.

I am reminded of a story I once heard about hockey star Bobby Hull. His team had lost, but he was over-heard singing in the shower after the game. When he emerged in a cheerful mood, someone challenged him: "How can you be so happy when we lost?" Bobby's reply: "Hey, I wish we had won

> *The fact is that there will always be variables, like weather, or the economy, which are beyond our immediate control. All you can ever do, or give, is your best.*

and I am concerned that we didn't, but I played one of the best games of my life today. I'm choosing to celebrate that fact."

Instead of celebrating like Bobby, I had become preoccupied with the fact that no one including my coaches and teammates had noticed my performance; I simply sulked.

Over time, I was able to gain some perspective, and I now realize I should have celebrated my first "unofficial" World Cup victory at Val Gardena. My performance was a personal validation that I was both capable and deserving of a first place finish. It was proof of eventual victory, even though the victory did not happen on that occasion.

As it turned out, I had a few more tough breaks that same season and on several occasions I needed to remind myself of my commitment to celebrate my performance, for intrinsic reasons, not let my self-esteem rely solely on external recognition of my performance. For example, at one point in the season, at a race in Wengen, Switzerland, I was leading the competition by 0.8 of a second—a huge margin, when an official stopped my run, concerned about a sudden obstruction that had appeared further down the course.

Having tired myself out and worn off much of the wax on my skis, I ended up posting a result just 35/100th of a second behind the winner of the event.

I knew that the only thing under my control that day, or any other day, was my performance, and it had been fantastic. The weather, the environment, accidents, and luck are all factors over which I have no control. At Wengen, I didn't waste any time moping. I bounced back quickly and concentrated on giving each race my best effort. Eventually it all paid off. I ended up winning a World Cup Championship and setting a downhill speed record that has yet to be broken!

Since my skiing days, I have realized how getting upset about things over which we have no control is simply a recipe for stress. This kind of unhealthy stress leads to a loss of ability to maintain a positive attitude and a dismal downward spiral in our performance. Once our performance has sunk to match the level of our lousy attitude, we fuel our frustration

> *Since my skiing days, I have realized how getting upset about things over which we have no control is simply a recipe for stress.*

over posting yet another less than stellar performance. If we don't recognize what we're doing, our attitude can become even more toxic and it only serves to continue to undermine our performance ability. The downward spiral continues!

Conversely, we can break this downward cycle by recognizing that there are many factors or performance variables that remain beyond our control. We can learn to stop wasting our energy in worrying about such variables and instead harness this same energy in the service of all that we can control—our performance! If we can do this, we can hope to hold more realistic expectations for ourselves and certainly, we'll derive a greater enjoyment from the journey.

This isn't necessarily easy stuff to wrestle with. I'd estimate that at least, weekly, I'm faced with a situation or circumstances I wish were different. I have to remind myself, repeatedly so, to take a step back and take stock of what is and isn't within my control. The hard part for me, as I suspect it is for many others, is letting go, in surrendering to the reality that I can't control everything, such as the behavior and feelings of others. The moment I remember to let go of such things, I experience a sense of peace within myself. Often, too, the problem situation or circumstance works itself out.

How does the desire to control show up or express itself in your life? Do you ever find yourself focusing on factors that can negatively impact your performance ability and which are also out of your control? When you dwell on such factors and your less than ideal outcomes, do you become angry? Has your anger ever done you any good?

I challenge you to build an inventory of all the variables that might be affecting your business results. For example, economic variables, market momentum, the corporate culture or staffing issues within a client's organization, time management, fatigue, written and oral communication skills, etc. Now classify these variables according to those over which you have some control and those over which you have no control. A shift in the economy, for instance, is something over which you have no control; conversely, how you choose to manage your time, or how much sleep you get, are both factors over which you do have a large measure of control.

Now here's the tricky part—to focus your energy and efforts only on the factors and variables you can control. When you evaluate your performance according to the things you can control, do so intrinsically, in terms of how well you performed, not according to any external recognition, validation, or reward.

Make a habit of celebrating the smaller as well as the larger achievements. Over a lifetime, there will always be more small achievements than large, which are just as worthy of celebration.

Don't always base a decision to celebrate your achievements upon external criteria. Make a habit of celebrating the smaller as well as the larger achievements. Over a lifetime, there will always be more small achievements than large, which are just as worthy of celebration but pass unnoticed by anyone else, other than those who are closest to you. Make sure you celebrate those occasions when you knock the ball out of the park, even if nobody else notices! Eventually, they will!

5.3

The Secret Information On Winning That Only Athletes Know

What To Do When You Are Not A Born Winner
The Process Of Producing Winning Results

Imagine walking proudly behind your country's flag in the opening ceremonies of your first World Cup competition. How do you think you would feel?

Goose bumps prickled the skin on my neck and my heart thumped with excitement, pride, and anticipation. I had been dreaming about this day for 12 years. What was about to happen here would change my life radically and forever. I thought I'd come prepared for anything, but really, I had no idea!

The next day I learned I had a starting position at the back, number 93. I crossed the finish line and looked up to see my result—83rd place. I looked at the scoreboard again and saw that ten racers before me hadn't finished. That meant I finished dead last! While there were still four more racers to come, to my disappointment, all four bettered my result. I was still last!

In disbelief I rechecked my time. Not only was I in last place, but 12 seconds separated my performance from that of the leader. Skiing is a sport where the difference between winning and losing is a matter of just a few hundredths of a second. My result was the equivalent of having lost a football game 180-0. My shoulders slumped forward and my dream of winning a World Cup never felt more unattainable.

When I thought about phoning home to tell my parents the disappointing news, I felt sick to my stomach. As I watched the interval times being handed out to all of the racers, I dreaded everyone seeing my name in last position. I was so embarrassed to come in last, and by such a significant margin, I wanted to crawl under a rock and hide.

Doubt plagued me and I asked myself, "Do I have what it takes to be a World Cup Champion, or have I been kidding myself all along?"

I didn't dare look at the split times (the interval times). Yet, with years of professional sports training and being conditioned to assess my performance, I felt compelled to review the data and try and figure out why I was so slow. I noticed that I lost 9 seconds on the easiest part of the course—the flat section. I had been focusing all my efforts on improving my time through the core technical sections, like the turns and the jumps, and I had all but ignored the easier ones. The difficult sections required me to work hard and tightly control my reactions, whereas the easier sections required me to execute a smoother, more relaxed technique called "gliding."

There was just one problem—I had never been a good glider.

Gliding is a technique applied to reduce friction between your skis and the snow, best achieved by letting the skis follow the fastest line down the slope and resisting any tendency to use your edges. It requires surrender and flow, not raw power or forced maneuvers. Good gliding technique feels effortless and not at all like hard work.

No wonder I ignored it.

I decided it was time to work on becoming a better glider and I asked one of the National Team coaches for his assistance. What he told me shook me to the core. "I'm sorry Cary, but either you're born a glider or you're not. You can't really do much to develop that ability."

The weight of his words struck me hard. If I wasn't able to master this skill, my chances of moving from the bottom ranks seemed slim. I was left wondering how I could become the best in the world if I couldn't learn to glide.

I felt hopeless and desperate. I wandered off, thinking, "This simply isn't fair. Why are some people born with the skill of gliding? All this time I'd been operating under the belief that hard work would reap the results I desired. But, all along, the winners had been those people who had worked hard but also possessed the good fortune to have been born with the ability to glide well. Was I destined never to be a great downhill skier, something I'd wanted so badly and worked so hard to achieve?"

To make matters worse, I'd discovered the consequences of this disappointing race were that I had not been selected to join the National Team. I was to return to complete the season with the Provincial Team. It felt like I had taken a giant step backwards.

Max Gartner, the Provincial Team coach, sat down with me to discuss my performance at the World Cup event. He asked me to share my strategy for becoming a better glider. As I heard his words, my heart sank.

"Why do you look so deflated when I mention gliding?," Max asked. "I've never been able to glide well and the National Team coach told me, either you're born a glider or you're not! I guess I've been thinking he may be right—as I've never been able to figure it out." Max's eyes flashed with a fierce look of determination. "Cary, I believe that you can learn just about anything you set your mind to. Why would gliding be any different than any other skill you've learned?" I stammered, "But he's an authority and he said … ." Max quickly interrupted, "You need to decide that it is possible for you to glide. You and I both know that you need to be a good glider to become a championship contender. Given what you are faced with, what do you think would be the best mindset to adopt? Is gliding something you believe you can learn and master or not?"

For a split second I felt utterly confused. Was it possible that the coach from the National Team was wrong? At my core, I took solace in Max's words. They also felt true. I realized I had a choice and a role in what I believed. I could choose to believe the National Team coach or I could choose to believe Max. I could choose to believe I had the capacity to learn to glide or not, and either way I would get to be right. I chose to believe that I could learn to be a great glider. In doing so I made manifest my belief in my ability to develop myself.

After interviewing many of the world's top gliders and working hard on improving my own gliding, I had another chance to race at a World Cup event at the end of the following season. When I crossed the finish line on that occasion, my performance placed me 35th in the world, just 3.5 seconds behind the winner. With this result, I was assured of a spot on the National Team and the World Cup circuit for the following

> *Our beliefs shape our reality. We can choose our beliefs in a way that guides our future or in a way that destroys our dreams. It is entirely our choice.*

year. I was ecstatic over having made such a quantum leap forward.

When I think about gliding now, I know that Max knew something at the time that I had yet to figure out—our beliefs shape our reality. We can choose our beliefs in a way that guides our future or in a way that destroys our dreams. It is entirely our choice. Max and I accomplished much during our year together because we both chose to believe in my potential development.

There are some skills with which we appear to be born, others we seem to acquire with relative ease, and still others which prove more difficult for us to master. In the end, skill acquisition seems to me to be less about whether something is initially difficult or easy for us to learn and more about our belief in our own abilities to learn anything we turn our minds to. I have since created a mantra: "If I'm not born with it, I can learn it or earn it."

Think about how often you have heard people say "Well, you're either born a leader or you're not. You're either born a salesperson or you're not. You're born with people skills or you're not. You're born with a good body or you're not." Indeed, we've probably said similar things about ourselves. I doubted my ability to learn to glide, and yet once I gave myself permission, I became one of the best during my tenure on the Word Cup circuit.

Our belief in our own abilities to learn and develop is critical to our ability to win. When we compare ourselves to others who appear to have an easier time of it, we can too quickly become discouraged, thinking, "it is just not in the cards for me." We end up becoming a victim of our present circumstances and render ourselves powerless to change or feel in control. When we hold ourselves back from advancing our own growth and learning, at best, we can expect our results to stay the same. More likely, our results will deteriorate.

> *In the end, skill acquisition seems to me to be less about whether something is initially difficult or easy for us to learn and more about our belief in our own abilities to learn anything we turn our minds to.*

On the other hand, when we believe we can learn the skills and techniques that enhance our ability to win, then we unleash more of our true potential. With this belief we are more likely to continue to search for the approaches and the solutions that will lead us to achieve better results. We begin working with what we've got instead of wishing we had something more. As we develop our skills, our results naturally improve. Occasionally, we will blast past incremental growth and make a quantum leap forward in our development.

How many times have you managed to convince yourself that you are unable to learn something at which you wanted to excel? Were you not born a great salesperson? Not born a great leader? Not born with a flair for numbers? Not born wealthy? Not born with a better physique? You can learn how to acquire these things in your life. It is possible for you to learn How to Win in any area of your life.

Pick one aspect of your present life situation in which you have been holding back and apply my mantra, "If I'm not born with it, then I can learn it or earn it."

To make it easier, surround yourself with as many people—like Max Gartner—as you can who believe in your potential and will encourage you to strive for the results and the life that you desire.

Notes To Yourself

5.4

Stop Whining And Start Winning

Redefining The Competitive Advantage

Without being seen, I made my way off the ski run and into the trees, out of plain sight. I took the ski pole in my right hand and brought it around in an arc towards the trunk of the pine four feet in front of me. With snow falling from the branches and most of the pole still intact, I took another step closer to the tree.

Winding up for another vigorous baseball bat swing, I broke what remained of my pole into two pieces. In my hand was a section less than a third of the original length of the pole, but just long enough to break over my knee. I proceeded to do just that.

I was still breathing the hard, short breaths of pent up anger. Somehow, breaking one pole just wasn't enough to dissipate my frustration. I grabbed the other pole that lay beside me in the snow, picked it up, and repeated the process of destruction. With ski pole shrapnel scattered around me, I looked down at my skis.

With the physical exertion, my sadness began to surpass my frustration. Half-sitting, half-falling on my side, I sat in the snow and began sobbing into my gloves.

I had spent more than half my life short life and a great deal of my parents' money on financing my dream of becoming a world-class downhill skier. Thus far, I had always felt my time and energy and parents' investment had been well spent. The results on the scoreboard that day told a different story.

I had just finished a Canadian Alpine Series ski race at Silver Star in Vernon, British Columbia. My performance had been, at best, average. I was disappointed with my result but had been able to console myself with the knowledge that many of the other racers were experienced competitors. Some skiers, in their mid-twenties had been racing for a decade. To race in the Canadian Alpine Series, you had to be at least fifteen and I was just sixteen myself.

After my run, I hung around the finish line watching the balance of the skiers post their results. Most of the racers after me were younger and posed little threat to my ranking. The scoreboard showed me in seventeenth place; not a great result, to be sure, but I figured my position wouldn't change with the balance of younger skiers still to come.

You might be asking, "Cary, was a seventeenth place result the reason for your pole breaking rage which ended in tears?"

In part, perhaps it was, but much of my anger and frustration had arisen out of witnessing fifteen-year-old Edi Podivinsky come down the slope and finish third. His result had undermined my belief that I had it in me to become a world-class skier. At sixteen, the age gap between us felt huge; he seemed like a child. That day however, his performance put him on the podium with the big boys.

What made matters a whole lot worse was that Edi had finished three and a half seconds ahead of me. In ski racing, a 1.5 second split between time scores is considered the equivalent of winning a 100-yard dash by 10 yards. Young Edi had done the sprinting equivalent of beating me by almost 25 yards!

First there had been the shock and shame of it all, and then my pole breaking rage. Having my clock cleaned so definitively by someone my junior caused me to question my abilities and doubt my dreams in such a fundamental way. My gut started to heave and I thought I was going to be sick.

For the first time in my ski career I seriously considered calling it quits. I thought to myself, "Who am I kidding, other than my parents and myself, who thinks that I could ever be the best in the world when I got lapped by boy wonder here?" Edi's result simply awakened the voice of the skeptic inside me; the voice that told me all my efforts were pointless.

If you've ever experienced giving something your all and then losing—horrifically—you'll understand my devastation. As I looked at Edi, I felt I knew what a future world champion looked like.

There was no question Edi was showing world championship potential and, if I continued to ski race, I would have front row tickets to watch his brilliant career unfold. What could be worse?

Then a realization hit me, "Do I watch Edi win the World Cup on television or is there a way I can learn from him and, perhaps, someday stand

> *In that early race with Edi I had made the near-fatal but very human mistake of using the result, the outcome, to define my future ability and potential.*

on the podium beside him? What if Edi is a gift, a gift that no coach, cash, or training camp can ever replicate?"

As amazing as this may sound, in a very short time, I moved from wallowing in the snow over Edi's exceptional ability, to recognizing that having repeated opportunities to observe his talent could become a significant training tool in support of my own development.

Although Edi and I continued to compete together, over the years we were able to help each other improve by sharing our best practices. Edi did become one of the best training tools and resources during the early years of my ski-racing career.

Several years later, the imagined event happened; both Edi and I stood side by side on the podium at a World Cup race. Together we achieved a significant skiing milestone by placing first and second for Canada; A one-two for Canada had been accomplished only once before.

I credit Edi for much of my success; without his fantastic abilities, I am confident I wouldn't have made it to the top of the world rankings in downhill skiing. You might imagine my shock at the press conference, when I announced my retirement from professional sport, Edi made the following statement: "Everything I've ever learned and everything I've ever achieved in this sport is because I was chasing Cary Mullen." I had always thought it was me chasing Edi, not the other way around!

Looking back, I realize how profound a lesson fifteen-year-old Edi had unknowingly taught me. You see, in that early race with Edi I had made the near-fatal but very human mistake of using the result, the outcome, to define my future ability and potential.

My momentary lack of belief in my own abilities to achieve my potential and fulfill my dreams, had been projected onto Edi. His superior result that day made me feel that he would be the one to crush my

> *I now believe that success in life is more about being involved in a grand game of leapfrog wherein I leap over you towards my goals and you leap over me towards yours.*

dreams. Initially, I had been unable to recognize that Edi could actually help me win. I was one of a few fish in a relatively small pond. Competing alongside Edi would help me maintain the momentum necessary to become the biggest fish in the ocean.

What if those around us whom we believe are standing between us and everything we've ever wanted, are not in our lives to prevent us from experiencing triumph, but instead exist to move us forward towards our goals? I now believe that success in life is more about being involved in a grand game of leapfrog wherein I leap over you towards my goals and you leap over me towards yours. At the end of the game, we've both moved forward and we've both won.

I wonder if you have ever blamed or are now blaming a lack of belief in yourself or in your ability to achieve success on someone close to you. How could you start to see such people as gifts? Is this person someone who you could play leapfrog with? What could that game of leapfrog do for your results?

5.5

How Excited Are You About Your Life?

Learn How To Renew Your Energy And Motivation

I stood alone outside our lodgings and I watched the rookie skiers walk by. Enthusiasm sparkled in their eyes. Laughter and joy filled the air around them. As a group, they vibrated with energy and excitement about the newness of their adventure. For the time being, they were blissfully unaware of what they did not yet know. Conversely, I was lacking that same spark. I was feeling less than enthusiastic about the forthcoming training camp.

Watching the rookies, I tried to remember what it had felt like to be in that position. I remembered feeling a similar joy and passion for training camp. I remember being filled with energy and excitement, and having a sparkle in my eye. As a rookie, I also remembered looking up to the veterans on the team and wondering what had happened to undermine their enthusiasm and excitement for training camp.

Now I was one of those veterans with the dull eyes. Twelve years of coming to Mt. Hood, Oregon had left me bored and frustrated. I had become an energy sinkhole, witnessing the energy and life drain out of me, and sometimes guilty of sucking it out of those around me.

My poor attitude was clearly having a negative impact on my performance. I didn't win as many training runs as I'd anticipated or hoped for, and I'd posted results which placed me in the middle of the pack far too often during the camp. Furthermore, I was not looking forward to another—rapidly approaching—training camp that was scheduled to take place at high altitude in Chile. Three weeks of training at 12,000 feet inevitably resulted in the loss of hard-earned muscle mass and I wasn't exactly happy about the unavoidable weight loss.

I knew I had to do something to reignite my enthusiasm. As another happy-go-lucky rookie walked past me, I was struck with a bright idea.

Being among the best and fastest of the racers on the team, I was one of the chosen few who had the privilege of choosing a room and his roommates. On the spot, I decided I would room with rookies while in Chile in the hope that their enthusiasm and energy would rub off on me.

We were three to a room and I chose to share the space with two rookies—Luke and a team member, Ryan, whom everyone referred to as 'The Kid.' Both Luke and The Kid were completely enamored with the beauty of Chile and the Andes mountains. The impressive glaciers, the abundant sunshine, and the exotic-looking Argentinean women had them buzzing with excitement. It was indeed contagious. Seeing the world through their eyes re-motivated me.

After we had settled into our quarters, I announced a roommates meeting. "We have to solve the weight loss problem," I said. "Every year I've been here, I end up leaving 10 pounds under weight, and I would welcome any assistance you can offer so that I can control and minimize the issue."

Luke and The Kid accepted the challenge with enthusiasm and lost no time in working on weight-retention strategies. After a day of training on the glaciers, instead of heading back to our room to catnap, as I had done during previous training camps, we headed out on something of a scavenger hunt to find materials with which we could fashion free weights and barbells. The three of us worked out every day in an effort to retain muscle mass rather than lose it. We found and repurposed empty gallon containers and broken broom sticks to suit our training purposes. It was crude, but effective, and fun. The rookies even built a chin-up bar.

We went into town and purchased boxes of pasta and ketchup. It sounds disgusting, but the ketchup was more like tomato paste and it tasted just fine after a hard workout. We ate an extra meal of pasta and sauce each day and consumed additional protein powder all in an attempt to maintain our muscle mass.

All through the camp I was more engaged and excited to be there. Not

We can't always rely only on ourselves for motivation. Sometimes we need to look to others for motivation and energy. We need to surround ourselves with positive people.

only had the rookies' enthusiasm rubbed off on me as I had hoped, we achieved our intended goal of weight maintenance. In fact, I even gained two pounds.

When we can remember to look for what is exciting and motivating, we'll inevitably see the world from a more positive perspective and we feel reinvigorated.

On leaving the camp at Mt. Hood, Oregon, I had felt bored and burned out. Contrary to my expectations, after training in Chile, I felt re-motivated. The fires had been rekindled inside of me. I learned that we can't always rely only on ourselves for motivation. Sometimes we need to look to others for motivation and energy. We need to surround ourselves with positive people.

When we can remember to look for what is exciting and motivating, we'll inevitably see the world from a more positive perspective and we feel reinvigorated. Gaining a fresh perspective energizes us and we can expect to experience an improvement in our performance ability and our subsequent results.

I challenge you to look at your present circumstances. Are there aspects of your own life over which you lack enthusiasm, energy, or joy? If so, what could you change or approach differently in order to enjoy life more fully? Do you surround yourself with energy givers or energy suckers? Have you become an energy sucker? If you feel you have, it might be time for you to discover your own version of 'rooming with the rookies'!

Notes To Yourself

5.6

Laziness As A Competitive Advantage

What Happens When We Stop Fighting And Start Flowing?

Standing in my hotel room, fingers clenched in my hair, I stared at the television screen. I'd been staring at it for most of the past two hours. Red faced with anger, I stewed and I dwelled. Anger was eating away at me. I was miserable and it was completely my own fault.

I was watching a video recording of the final ski training run for a North American Championship race, a run in which a teammate had beaten me. Despite my competitive nature, his win wouldn't have been such a big deal if he hadn't been regarded as the laziest member of our current roster.

Not only had he beaten me, but he had done so soundly, by a significant margin. I cannot express the fury that I felt in losing to Brian. It wasn't just his fellow teammates who believed him to be lazy; it was the general consensus among the coaches as well. Brian actually appeared to be proud of his admitted slothful behaviors. Where was the justice?

I felt I gave 100%, day in and day out, training hard and racing hard. I consistently pushed myself to succeed. And here was Brian, a guy who didn't seem to care very much, who often didn't show up for practice and when he did, certainly didn't exert himself as much as I did. It felt so unfair and I was almost consumed by my burning animosity toward him.

Alone in my room, I watched the video footage for as long as I could stand to do so. As I tried to regain some perspective, I began to wonder. How on earth had Brian beaten me? What was he doing that could be so different from my own regime that could garner him a better result?

The simplicity of the question I needed to ask suddenly dawned on me: "What was Brian doing that I wasn't yet seeing?" In asking myself this question, I had allowed myself to admit that Brian was doing something better than I was.

I watched the video over again from this different perspective and studied his race and then my own for two further hours. As I watched Brian, I noticed that he seemed incredibly relaxed as he skied down the hill. His performance looked almost lackadaisical. I, on the other hand, looked like I was fighting the mountain, fighting gravity, even fighting myself. My face was tight. My teeth were clenched. Every movement looked forced.

Watching Brian was like watching syrup flow across a pancake—it was just smooth and easy. Watching the footage of my race performance the very antithesis of Brian's performance was—it just looked painful.

As I studied Brian's form, I began to gain a new appreciation for his approach. He not only flowed down the mountain but he looked like he was enjoying himself. I spent the rest of that evening working on visualizing my own flowing performance with the intention of putting it all to work the following day. I practiced flowing, relaxing, and letting go of the fight during my training runs. You'll never believe what happened.

I won my first North American Championship! But more importantly than the race result, I learned a valuable lesson. I learned to flow and relax, both skills that did not come very easily for me. It would be a lesson I would work hard to perfect. Furthermore, I also learned an invaluable lesson about teamwork—to look for people's strengths and learn from them.

Behaviorally, it seems we draw attention to the weaknesses and deficits in others with greater frequency than we ever talk about strengths and attributes. I'm not sure why, but perhaps because it is easier or maybe it's part of our genetic programming for survival (to seek out the weak of the species). Maybe it's symptomatic of the often critical nature of society and a component of the media that feeds on sensationalizing other people's problems and shortcomings. Maybe it makes the rest of us feel better, albeit temporarily, to focus

> *Behaviorally, it seems we draw attention to the weaknesses and deficits in others with greater frequency than we ever talk about strengths and attributes.*

on the faults of others as opposed to our own. Regardless, looking for the problems rather than for what is working just seems easier.

Despite the difficulty we have with the process, it is to our ultimate advantage, if we look for the strengths in others. When we focus on seeking out other people's strengths, not only are we more appreciative of them, we may also be able to emulate these strengths to improve our own performance.

> *When we focus on seeking out other people's strengths, not only are we more appreciative of them, we may also be able to emulate these strengths to improve our own performance.*

In discovering Brian's strength, I not only won a race but also was able to finally respect him for his hidden talents. Before realizing this, I had both wanted—and expected—my teammates to be just like me. How awful would that actually have been?

Think about it! If all of my teammates had been just like me, there would have been nothing for me to learn. The lesson I learned that day changed my attitude about working with people which, in turn, has changed the nature of my relationships. I now look for ways to capitalize on the strengths of others as opposed to focusing on their weaknesses.

Adopting a more appreciative attitude reduces the anger, frustration, and confusion that can arise in perceiving differences as weaknesses. Such an attitude also fosters the ability to see the unique brilliance in everyone. When you can leverage that brilliance to help improve your own performance—wow—it is amazing! As a further benefit, your relationships in general become stronger because you can genuinely respect and appreciate others and celebrate our differences. Look past the 'obvious weaknesses' of the members of your team and find their hidden strengths. Then learn from those strengths and you'll benefit from the diversity on your team.

It's your turn now. Think about a person in your life who is currently driving you crazy. Maybe it's a family member or maybe it's a co-worker. Make a list of their obvious weaknesses! I'm sure you'll find that task easy to

> *Look past the 'obvious weaknesses' of the members of your team and find their hidden strengths. Then learn from those strengths and you'll benefit from the diversity on your team.*

accomplish. Now make another list of their outstanding strengths. Harder to do, isn't it!? Persevere though because you are going to make a third list outlining what you could learn from this person? How could you learn from and make use of their strengths to better yourself? Repeat this exercise with every significant person in your life and your teamwork and results will flourish.

Thanks, Brian!

5.7

The Purpose Of Life

The One Thing We Avoid Doing That Can Make All The Difference

Trembling in my bed, I cried silently and prayed for the pain to subside. Terrified to make any noise and afraid that any movement would make it worse, I lay in a cold sweat and hoped I'd make it through till the morning.

Several weeks before, I'd suffered a severe concussion. I'd pushed too hard during a race and fallen badly. Holed up in the guest room at my parents' farmhouse, trying to take it easy and recover, I felt awful and worried that something terrible had gone undiagnosed. Perhaps an embolism had partially blocked an artery in my brain. The pain was so intense and unlike anything I had experienced before. I believed I might be dying. Terrified, I wondered if my ski-racing career had been worth it.

I began to reflect on my life. Myriad emotions flowed in and out of my thoughts: fear, anger, frustration, regret. If I wasn't going to make it through the night, had the life I'd lived been to any purpose? How had I got to this point? What had my life really been about? Did I really matter?

N that moment, I realized that I had been greatly blessed in having a positive relationship with my parents. I regretted that I hadn't shown more affection towards my mother. All my life she'd loved me unconditionally and I hadn't acknowledged or thanked her nearly enough for that gift. I made a vow to myself, should I make it through the night, I would show her more affection. I'd try to be fully present to her. I would find more frequent opportunities to give her a hug and I'd spend more time simply listening to her.

Lying perfectly still in an attempt to minimize the pounding in my head, I thought of my father and the wisdom he had shared with me. I thought about the sound and practical guidance he had given me over the years. I realized that the relationship I had with my father was the most precious of all the relationships I'd yet had in my all-too-short life. He was my best friend, and yet I had not told him how much he really mattered to me. Again, I vowed to do a better job of telling him how influential he'd been in my life.

Fortunately, I did make it through the night, and I remembered my vows. Can you believe that it took me a further twelve months before I made good on their implementation? It seems both ridiculous and a bit embarrassing. It took me a year to develop the habit of hugging my mother and telling my father that he mattered to me. Why is it so easy to avoid telling the people we love (and who love us) how important they are to us?

When I finally mustered up the courage to talk to my father, we were out driving around in the old family pick up truck. Behind the wheel with the road as comfort and the scenery passing us by, I told him about the night of my darkest hour, during my recuperation from the concussion in the farmhouse. I told him about my fear of dying and that among the things I would have regretted most was not telling him how important he'd been in my life. Tearing up, I told my dad that he was my best friend.

"Thanks Cary," my dad said, with tears in his eyes, "You made my day." He hesitated, still fighting back the tears as he said, "No, you just made my life."

I now take comfort in having had that conversation with my father and I know that it has made a difference for both of us to have said it.

Why did it take me a year to say that, and a year to hug my Mom? I I don't know why it is so hard for us to share our feelings with each other. I suppose we procrastinate over this just as we do with most everything else, believing that there will always be a better time, later on. As we occupy ourselves with doing the "important stuff" now, we overlook or avoid having the conversations that matter. We may also tell ourselves that the people closest to us already know how we feel about them, so we don't have to tell them—a handy excuse. Sometimes, our sense of pride holds us back, as the little voice in our head whispers, "Why should I go first—why haven't *they* ever shared what I mean to *them*?"

More often than not, though, what holds us back is the difficulty we routinely experience in breaking out of deeply entrenched patterns of behavior that we have established in our relationships. Out of habit, we fall into comfortable and predictable ways of being with others which are hard, if not impossible, to change. I think we conclude that if we stay where we are, and others stay where they are, then we will continue down a familiar path. It is a comfortable way of being. It is so comfortable in fact, that the very thought of changing the status quo in a relationship causes us stress and evokes uncertainty, even fear.

Taking risks in any primary relationship can evoke anxiety and fear because we are uncertain about the reaction we might receive. What if the other person laughs at me, or thinks I'm being melodramatic, or weak, or ridiculous? What if they stop liking me or figure out that I am unworthy of their love? Fear arising out of my uncertainty over how my behavioral changes would initiate the start of a different kind of relationship with my parents is why I held back on honoring my vows for so long. To experience fear in such circumstances seems reasonable. After all, such conversations of the heart do require courage, the same courage that lets us enter our own hearts.

The real tragedy is that we rob our loved ones of the opportunity to fully know who we are and how we feel about them.

What I know for sure is that our lives are about our relationships. They are our truest form of connection, purpose, and sense of immortality. Without meaningful relationships, a truly winning life is impossible.

I encourage you to look at your own life. What relationships do you value? What are you actively doing to make these relationships stronger? Think about someone you love and ask yourself, "What would I regret if I were never to see that person again?" Are you sharing your true feelings with the

> *What I know for sure is that our lives are about our relationships. They are our truest form of connection, purpose, and sense of immortality. Without meaningful relationships, a truly winning life is impossible.*

people who make a difference in your life? Does your family know how much you love them? Do your friends know how important they are to you? Are you sure?

It's difficult to have these conversations, I know, and it's anxiety provoking, but it is also worth the risk. Give yourself permission to be generous and share your feelings. Break out of old habits and reinvigorate your relationships. If you are committed to fostering and building the best possible relationships with those around you, don't let another day go by without telling the people in your world that they matter. Write your thoughts down in a letter if that's easier. Just do it.

One more request, to those of you who feel ready to take your relationships to a new level. I would love to hear how your bold, new conversation unfolded, and how you were received. Send an e-mail to me at **cary@carymullen.com** and let me know! Dare to share.

Now What? Focus Forward

I HAVE GREATLY ENJOYED SHARING THESE STORIES WITH YOU. I wish you well as you pursue your own continuing journey towards winning, wherever it may take you.

All of us, myself included, require something to remain motivated. It should now come as no surprise to you that the principle reason top performers remain at the top is because they apply their own set of strategies, all of which help them to maintain their focus. I would like to provide you with some ongoing support, to help you maintain your focus. We are, both of us, lifelong students of the pursuit of success and its attainment, and we are both committed to the continuing search for new lessons and strategies for How to Win. Thus, if you're interested in receiving further accounts of my most recent experiences and life lessons, I encourage you to register for *Winning Insights*, a series of online articles, short stories, strategies, and quick tips devoted to the process of winning. *Winning Insights* is published 26 times a year (every two weeks) and it is free! To register, send an e-mail to me at **cary@carymullen.com** with *Winning Insights* in the title, or visit us at **www.carymullen.com** and register to begin receiving *Winning Insights* straight away.

Winning Insights is issued on a regular basis for a reason. Have you ever established a goal but then failed to achieve it? What went wrong? What might have been missing? Usually, it is our failure to consistently focus on our intended goal or target. Without an established system of regular check-ins, it is easy to lose that focus. Without some external support and motivation, it is just as easy to become distracted or discouraged, either or both of which can undermine our faith in our thoughts and our commitment to taking action. We lose belief in ourselves and our ability to achieve our goals. We pay the price for drifting. In the end, we fail to achieve as many of our goals as we might, and consequently we do not live out the life we have dreamed of or imagined. For those of you who feel you are successful in goal setting and establishing targets, and judge yourself to be highly focused, with the right tools at your fingertips, it is still possible to hone your skills, sharpen that focus, and achieve better results. Routine habits and typical patterns of behavior may not always work to help us reach our goals.

If you are looking for proven tools and guided activities focused on winning, then I strongly encourage you to also consider working through the *How to Win Success System.*

This interactive, five-module, multimedia self-development program has been designed to help you achieve even more success. It is a comprehensive program of self-development intended to overhaul your entire life, eliminate negative habits and beliefs, and provide you with all of the tools you require in order to succeed. The exercises and coaching tips presented in the *How to Win Success System* will help you to incorporate the five *Winning Secrets*™ and make them an integral part of your winning life. By e-mailing me at cary@carymullen.com and requesting your HOW to WIN coupon, you will be eligible to purchase the *How to Win Success System* for $227 instead of the usual $297; a savings of $70. If you are serious about creating more enduring success and would like more information, visit us at **www.carymullen.com** and look under *How to Win Success System* to review the system for yourself.

I believe everything we need to know about winning is out there for us to discover and learn from, just as long as we stay open to innovation and remain committed to the journey. I invite you to embrace all that I have shared with you and encourage you to take what you now know about the five *Winning Secrets*™ and recommit to your passion and enthusiasm for a winning life.

I applaud your dedication and commitment in your pursuit of better results and, ultimately, a better life. The questing spirit in me salutes the winning spirit within you. Racer ready ... Go!

What's Next?

A FTER A SUCCESSFUL SKIING CAREER—culminating in the achievement of winning a World Cup downhill competition as well as being a two-time Olympian, becoming a leader in the competitive world of keynote speakers, having considerable success in the real estate industry, and most recently publishing *How to Win*, what's the next step for Cary Mullen?

He's building a dream resort on the ocean for active, family-oriented people. How did he come to this? Real estate has long been of interest for Cary, and an early passion that saw him obtain his Real Estate License in his native province of Alberta, Canada at the age of 21. Studying and obtaining his license was an obvious path by which Cary acquired some greater knowledge and professional development in the field of real estate. From the outset, he displayed an enviable knack for anticipating market trends, as he identified an winning opportunity and made a solid first property investment in Prince George British Columbia, despite receiving advise to the contrary. He doubled his money in just one year and was up and running. This market sense in real estate has stayed with Cary through numerous successful investments and developments in many areas of Western Canada including Prince George, Canmore, Banff, Strathmore, Edmonton and Calgary. His group of companies now owns and manages more than 100 properties and over 8,000 acres of real estate.

Despite all of this success, Cary knew his next step in the real estate industry needed to be with a project that would be both inspiring and rejuvenating and in a tropical location that he and his family could enjoy year round. As a leading keynote speaker, Cary has taken full advantage of his opportunities for international travel these past seven years. He has visited and experienced many wonderful tourist destinations including paces as far flung as Prague in the Czech Republic, the Dominican Republic and Maui, all of which has enabled him to search for an ideal location for his next real estate venture.

After visits to 13 countries and some further research on another 20 countries as potential locations, Cary concluded Mexico represented his best choice for both lifestyle and real estate investment opportunities. All of the research and travel enabled Cary to develop a comprehensive checklist of 44 criteria or factors to consider when purchasing retirement, recreation or investment property. On three separate scouting trips to Mexico Cary traveled throughout Cancun and the Caribbean coast, the Yucatan Peninsula, some of Baja, California and the entire Pacific coast, and upon arriving in the community of Puerto Escondido he realized he found the spot.

His first real estate acquisition was a beautiful ocean front villa both for his own families' enjoyment as well as a business development opportunity through exclusive luxury rentals. When Cary purchased the villa it was known as *La Morena*, which means dark skinned woman in Spanish. With new ownership, it seemed appropriate to rename the home so Cary's wife, Kristina asked some of the locals for ideas and, they voted for *Casa Rubia* which is Spanish for "blonde house." With Cary, Kristina, and their three children all having blonde hair it was an appropriate choice.

Spending no less than nine weeks of rejuvenating vacation time at Casa Rubia each year and with the villa now operating as a successful vacation rental property, Cary turned his attention to purchasing a large piece of ocean front property for his dream resort. Cary's plan to create a resort in Mexico was ambitious, but his idea of creating a destination that would provide investors with a desirable lifestyle was really at the heart of his vision. He envisioned a community where family and friends could enjoy fun, fitness, rejuvenation, access to business services, personal and professional development, great socializing and a philanthropic initiative to give back to the community.

Vivo Resorts has been planned with these core attributes at the forefront of all development plans and decision making to ensure Cary's vision is not compromised. It's a place to live fully and to find greater life balance with those that you care about. Not only will Vivo Resorts enrich the lives of those who choose to be a part of it, it will undoubtedly become a significant component in the net worth of any investors' portfolio. If you are interested in enhancing your lifestyle and owning your own piece of oceanfront property, consider Cary Mullen's oceanfront resort at **www.VivoResorts.com**. Alternatively, to get a taste for the region and enjoy the vacation destination of a lifetime, consider his luxurious oceanfront mansion which can be reviewed at **www.CasaRubia.com**.

Notes To Yourself

_____

_____

_____

_____

_____

_____

_____

_____

_____

_____

_____

_____

_____

_____

_____

_____

_____

_____

_____

_____

_____

_____

_____

_____

_____

_____

_____

Afterword

by Lorne Mullen

W HEN CARY FIRST ASKED ME TO WRITE the afterword for this book, I was both surprised and honored. I was surprised because I believe that there are many other people who know far more about winning than I do, and who would be better qualified to write these closing comments. Cary has led a unique life, one which has enabled him to meet people who know him by name, including Prince Albert of Monaco, Wayne Gretzky, Picabo Street, a number of CEO's from *Fortune 500* companies as well as one or two billionaires. After all, as his father I am simply a retired educator and a farmer-at-heart. To have asked me, Cary must believe that raising a world champion makes me a natural authority on winning.

Beyond being surprised at Cary's request to write his afterword, I have to admit that I was deeply flattered. I believe that one of the greatest compliments a parent can receive is to have your child ask you to do something like this for them. It has been an honor to witness the unfolding of the person Cary has become. Every day, he gives me new reasons to be proud of him. While I don't have the words to describe the experience of parenting a son with such determination and wisdom, I can speak to my certainty that Cary has created a path to winning that all of us would be wise to follow.

I believe that Cary has captured just about everything there is to know about winning in his five *Winning Secrets*™, yet his greatest contribution to the field of winning is his strength of character. To Cary, winning has never been "winning" unless it has been achieved in the right way. In skiing, weather would often play a role on any given day, in who was able to record the fastest time on the course. If the first half of the group had to deal with wind or a storm and he didn't, Cary would perceive that as an unfair advantage and wouldn't have enjoyed his victory or his better result as fully. Cary receives no satisfaction from success unless it is accomplished fairly, where everyone has done his or her best.

As a child, his strength of character was evident when he struggled with his small stature. Cary was participating in a sport where physical size is an advantage and yet he was small for his age. A small physique didn't stop him. His persistence led him to make the decision at the age of twelve to leave our family—so he might attend a sports academy —to develop his overall athletic abilities. He stayed for three years! Cary's belief was that he could learn how to succeed in spite of his physical challenges. His dream and persistence were more powerful than any obstacle such as his size.

I think his strength of vision is why it is so important for Cary to share the lessons that he has learned. Cary lives his life with the belief that if he can accomplish success, then anyone can; and he wants to help you get there. In a world where it is easy to get lost in consumption and achievement, Cary has never forgotten his core values. He genuinely cares about the success of others and he wants to make his life and work a benefit to others. Once he sets his mind to something, then watch out, this kid is determined!

From a very young age, perhaps as early as three years, Cary seemed to have an awareness of who he was and where he was going. By the age of six, he would race down the ski slope visualizing himself winning a World Cup—someday. As he would cross his imaginary finish line at the bottom of the run, Cary would throw his arms up in the air and scream "yeah!," pretending he had just captured the title "best skier in the world." At the time, we had to hold back our smiles, yet after witnessing a little more than twenty years of hard work, Cary's prophecy came true when he was crowned the World Cup Downhill Champion in Aspen, Colorado in 1994.

In hindsight, I realize that Cary was born to do the work he is presently undertaking: he has always been a natural storyteller. When Cary was a child, it was important for our family to have dinners together—which we achieved most evenings. While Cary could be quite serious at times, it was over family suppertime that he would entertain us with stories from his day at school. He had a way of not merely making meaning out of his experiences, but seeing the humor in every situation. There were many nights he had us roaring with laughter.

As his father, I can tell you that Cary speaks from the heart, he speaks from experience, and he speaks with the genuine intention of helping others. He truly lives the life that he talks about and he applies his five *Winning Secrets*™ in to his own life every day.

I hope that in sharing his winning experiences, lessons, and moments of clarity that you will be able to learn from them. Perhaps better still, I hope you will use these experiences, together with Cary's five *Winning Secrets*™, to help you to achieve all that you have ever dreamed of achieving.

Lorne Mullen
Strathmore, Alberta
March, 2007

Thematic Story Index

Quick Guide To Themes

Cluster 1: Overcoming Negative Beliefs
- Held Back By Your Beliefs
- Struggling With The Need To Be Perfect
- Unsure Whether You Can Learn How To Win
- Unsure How To Assess Your Performance

Cluster 2: Living Life to the Fullest
- Taking Life Too Seriously
- Feeling Out Of Control
- Unable To Set Boundaries To Protect Yourself
- Being Held Back By Fear

Cluster 3: Making Decisions & Taking Action
- Choosing The Right Opportunity
- Frozen In Inaction
- Caught In Uncertainty
- Not Sure Whether To Trust Your Resources

Cluster 4: Finding Happiness in Life
- Fleeting And Sporadic Sense Of Happiness
- Feeling Like You Have Lost Perspective
- Defined by Achievements And Material Possessions
- Not Enjoying Life
- Unable To Let Go Of Stress In Tough Situations
- Taking Relationships For Granted
- Not Taking Risks In Your Relationships

Cluster 5: Focusing Your Attention
- Not Leveraging Your Strengths
- Trying To Be All Things To All People
- Dividing Your Efforts Between Multiple Focuses
- Not Preparing Enough (Or Effectively)

Cluster 6: Increasing Your Effectiveness
- Feeling Like You Could Be More Effective
- Lacking Energy
- Stuck In Old Habits
- Needing To Have All The Answers
- Unclear On Your Long-term Vision/Purpose
- Lacking Time

Cluster 7: Being Resilient
- Preparing for the Worst
- Feeling Like A Victim Of Circumstance
- Having A Hard Time Bouncing Back From Failure
- Having Trouble Admitting When You Have Made A Mistake
- Unable To Learn From Prior Mistakes
- Deciding When To Cut Your Losses
- Stuck Asking "Why Me?"

Cluster 8: Optimizing Your Team
- Overcoming Jealousy
- Handling Ruthless Competition
- Feeling Like You Have To Go It Alone
- Dealing With Someone Who Is Driving You Crazy

Guide To Stories

Cluster 3: Making Decisions & Taking Action

Cluster 4: Finding Happiness in Life

Cluster 5: Focusing Your Attention

Cluster 6: Increasing Your Effectiveness

Cluster 7: Being Resilient

Cluster 8: Optimizing Your Team

Acknowledgments

Y OU MIGHT BE WONDERING WHY the acknowledgments appear at the back of the book. Let me assure you that this isn't because I want to bury my thanks to all those people who have assisted with the publication of this book. Indeed, there are quite a number of people without whom this book would never have seen the light of day. As a reader, I typically skip over the acknowledgments. It is only after I have read the book, hopefully gained a few new insights and developed some personal sense of the author, that I have an interest in reading about those who assisted in bringing the book to fruition. Now that you have read my personal chronicles that have introduced you to many of the characters in my life, I think now might be a more appropriate time to express my gratitude for their many contributions.

To my creative team, consisting of Wendy Astle, Michelle Bellas, Colin Collard and Karen Harris, working with the four of you has made a significant, positive difference in my experience of creating this book. You have my complete admiration and appreciation!

To Wendy Astle for being my assistant and picking up all of the loose ends and many small details that can easily be left behind but make all the difference to eventual outcomes.

To Michelle Bellas for being my writing coach, providing creative input on the manuscript and helping to pull it all together. In the process of turning my experiences into compelling stories, you have helped me to find my "writing voice."

To Colin Collard for being the big ideas guy. You have been a never-ending source of crazy ideas, new knowledge, and pure inspiration. Thank you for continuing to bend my mind and raise my pulse.

To Karen Harris for driving the sales and logistics of my speaking business. Your attention towards this aspect of my business has freed me to devote my time attention towards other projects, like this book.

To all my agents and representatives at numerous speakers' bureaus, especially Jaime Cichon, Roz Cole, Christa Haberstock, Brian Lord, David

Loy, Martin Peremuller, Janice Scott, Matt Sherwood and Katrina Kaposts Smith—thank you all for facilitating opportunities for me to share my five Winning Secrets™ at live events and conferences around the world.

To my friends, colleagues, and teammates who have helped me to develop and evolve my theories about winning.

To Jordy Burks for helping me clarify my views, often through healthy dialogue and debate. You have helped me to clearly distinguish between what I know and what I have yet to learn. When I most needed it, thanks for being there to kick my butt!

To Vince Poscente for being a mentor in the professional speaking business and for sharing your own experiences as a writer. You are truly a champion and most generous in your support and assistance towards others—a champion among champions.

To my teammates, in particular Felix Belczyk, Rob Bosinger, Rob Boyd, Thomas Grandi, John Mealey, Chad Mullen, Graydon Oldfield, Edi Podivinsky, Luke Sauder, Murray Smith, Ralf Socher, Brian Stemmle, Darren Thorburn, and Roman Torn among many others. I acknowledge the privilege I have had in learning something about winning from each one of you. Thank you for sharing your time, expertise, and esprit de corps with me on our individual and collective journey to become the best in the world.

To all my amazing coaches, Dave Armstrong, Germain Barrette, Peter Bosinger, Reinhard Eberl, Max Gartner, Bruce Henry, Jon Kolb, Benoit Lalande, Dave Marchant, Mark Sharp, Terry Spence, Helmut Spiegel, Dale Stephens, Paul Venner, Ken Vogel, and Mike and Bonnie Wiegele. You have brought out the best in me. Thank you all for helping me to live into my potential more fully!

To my current life coaches and life training partners from the Vintage Leadership mastermind group: Colin Collard, Frank Lonardelli, Dennis Plintz and Lee Rogers. Thank you all for being my winning-life training partners and for helping me believe in my infinite potential. Each of you is a unique gift and all of you are inspiring. As our master coach and facilitator, a special thanks to Colin Collard. You have dared to lead me to a level of accomplishment above and beyond all previous awareness. Your coaching and facilitation skills place you among the best there are in the business.

There are also a few more people who deserve acknowledgement for their personal sacrifices made in support of this book.

To my wife Kristina for having patience with me during the course of this writing project that took place just after the birth of our second child, Linnea. Thank you for supporting me in this work, even when it meant late dinners, divided attention and the frequent, "it will just be a few more minutes" white lies.

To my parents, you have touched my life in profound ways. Your steadfast belief in me has enabled me to live life to my full potential. Without your unconditional love and support, the success I have achieved, including this book, would not have been possible.

To my brother Shawn, my sister Blais, and my other extended family members, thank you for taking time and making room to understand my dedication to that which drives me, which is something bigger and more profound and is often difficult to articulate.

Finally, my thanks to folks like you, many of whom made valuable suggestions and shared your ideas during the development of this book. Without your feedback regarding the impact my stories have had in your lives, it is most unlikely this project would ever have come to fruition. I salute each and every one of you for continuing your own quest for inspiration and new knowledge to enhance your own lives, your own ultimate success, and your own positive impact on the world. Thank you for giving me that collective nudge to lunge forward into writing these stories! They now belong to you.

Cary Mullen
Puerto Escondido, Mexico
March, 2007